Dorm Decor

DORM DECOR

Remake Your Space with
More than 35 Projects

By Theresa Gonzalez
and Nicole Smith
Photographs by Evan Sklar

CHRONICLE BOOKS
SAN FRANCISCO

Library of Congress-in-Publication Data:

Gonzalez, Theresa, 1972–
    Dorm Decor : remake your space
with more than 35 projects / by Theresa
Gonzalez and Nicole Smith ; photographs by
Evan Sklar.
        p. cm.
Includes index.
    ISBN: 978-0-8118-6347-6
    1. Textile crafts. 2. Handicraft.
3. House furnishings. 4. Dormitories.
I. Smith, Nicole, 1979- II. Title.
    TT699.G66 2009
    746—dc22
            2008010878

Manufactured in China

Designed by
Catherine Macken Bullimore

Illustrations digitized by
Jane Fay

10 9 8 7 6 5 4 3 2 1

Chronicle Books LLC.
680 Second Street
San Francisco, CA 94107
www.chroniclebooks.com

Contents

Introduction

Hey There, Crafty Coed!

Excited to move into your new room? It could be so many things: A cozy nest. Party central! Cinderblock city. (OK, sorry, dorm living isn't always that dire.) No matter how you imagine your new room, the point is, it's *yours!* How you decorate it and make it your perfect place for the next nine months is entirely up to you.

At first glance it's possible your new home-away-from-home may leave a little something to be desired. There's such a variety of university architecture and school-issued furnishings, there's no telling exactly what you might walk into. Who knows, it might be super-cute. But it might be underwhelming, and it definitely will be unadorned. In most cases, you'll find industrial flooring or high-traffic carpet, painted cinderblock or plaster walls, and lackluster (to say the least) furniture. There will be blank walls just begging for decorations, and windows awaiting treatment.

That's where we come in. We've got tons of fresh ideas and fun fabrics to upgrade those creepy carpets and bland walls with more than just tacked-up posters. Inside, you'll find reversible projects that change on a dime, hanging projects that free up valuable floor and desk space, and organizing projects that keep your room (and your life!) clutter-free. With clever ways to add color, light, and more room to your room, you can transform a no-frills dorm into fabulous digs.

We like to think of a small, undecorated space as an opportunity to get creative and dream up ways to make it better. Kids and candy stores come to mind. We've learned from studying interior design and working at craft and fashion magazines that going from blank box to comfy nest can happen quickly—and on a budget—when you want it to. For some projects in this book, all you need are scissors, some bold fabric, and a simple pattern (which we tucked into the pocket at back for you).

We give instructions for some machine-sewn projects, but also offer no-sew alternatives in case you don't have access to a machine at school. And there are lots of projects that upgrade store-bought items or your old bedroom duds with cool embellishments using our templates.

Most of the projects here are a breeze for beginners. Some are more challenging . . . but you're smart, you can handle them. If you can get through your SATs, you can get through this book. And, unlike the SATs, we let you cheat. If you find an easier, better, more "you" way to get it done, kudos to you. But in case you get stuck along the way, we've provided tips and tricks to help you get it right (see page 14). We've also bolded terms in our instructions that might be unfamiliar to you. Check out our glossary in the back for all the vocab.

So whether this is your first year at a big urban university or your third at a tiny school in the country, you owe it to yourself to make your room as beautiful, organized, and comfortable as you can. Here we show you how to do it yourself. Ever have an idea in your head of exactly what you want but no matter how long and wide you search, the stores just don't get it right? We give you the tools to make just what you're looking for. Try our projects, then invent your own. Crafting gives you the freedom to express yourself; it's not only fun, but rewarding, too. No matter how grand or simple, the efforts you make to decorate your room will change the way you feel when you wake up, when you arrive home from a long day, or when you're just lounging around with your friends.

That's the funny thing about a dorm room: It's a bedroom, office, and living room in one. That's a lot of QT in a small space, so it's important to make it function well in all its roles. Because you'll sleep, dress, study, entertain, and more within these four walls for the better part of a year, we divided this book by how you use the room. Decorate your bed and windows with pillows, lamps, and a whimsical curtain from our Where You Sleep section, organize your desk with items from Where You Study, host a dorm-room fête with party projects from Where You Hang Out, find cool toiletry trinkets in Where You Wash, and doll up in style with Where You Dress. Think of your dorm as your starter apartment, your mini loft, and your sanctuary from the stresses of balancing classes with friends, boyfriends, parties, and all the other fun of school.

In the end, it's all about putting your own personal style on your surroundings. Think about it: Why would you buy run-of-the-mill linens from the same place you buy your soap and tampons?! It can be much more satisfying to sew something, custommade, that no one else will have. Create (and think!) for yourself with projects that say free-thinker, not following-the-pack. Gather the girls (and crafty boys, we know you're out there) and take a creative leap—this is your chance to stand out from the cookie-cutter crowd. And come May, when it's time to pack up your things, you can take these tricks with you to next year's sanctuary.

Start fresh. Use your imagination. Have fun. And get crafting!

Moving In

Dealing with Cinderblocks and Storage

You have about 200 square feet, give or take, that you'll call home for the next nine months. This is your first school lesson: How do you make the most with the least? Think of it as a creative challenge—see how many cool things you can fit inside your room and still keep it comfortable. It's satisfying to discover how little space you really need. And take it from us, this knowledge comes in handy when you move on from dorms to apartments, where more space means more rent.

During your initial visit you'll get the chance to see an actual dorm room at your school. Take advantage of this time to find out the dimensions of the room and write down the amenities available. Take note of window measurements for curtains (see the quick measuring guide on page 31), available seating (we've got a Better Bean Bag on page 100 that you're going to love), and electrical outlets (a power strip and extension cord is always key when sharing a small space). If you're moving in sight unseen, try calling your school or visiting its Web site to find out about the room details so you know exactly what to expect and what to bring. Once you know what you're working with, we can help spruce it up with arty poster displays, brighter lighting projects, and fab fabrics to give your dorm the personal touch it most definitely deserves.

And by personal, we mean a breath of fresh *you* in what will most likely be a shared space. You want equal footing, and that means communicating with your co-dorm dweller. We can't stress enough how important it is to have that first phone conversation with her. It's the best way to avoid bringing duplicate items and wasting valuable space! (Check out our list of questions on the next page to guide the conversation.) You might try to coordinate your bedding, too. Discuss styles and tastes—you may be modern while she's more traditional—but you can coordinate with color. See our color section in the following pages to keep you, your roommate, and your room in harmony.

Keeping clutter to a minimum is also key—a cluttered space means a cluttered life. When packing at home, only bring items you love. You want to create as much open space as possible. It may seem like you have plenty of room at the beginning of the year, but class projects (and books) can start to pile up and take over. Working your way up, rather than out, is always best. Cinderblocks that you can use to elevate your bed can provide additional storage space below (and to doll them up we show you how to make a cute bookend [page 77] that you adapt into a cinderblock cozy). You can stow suitcases underneath and use that luggage to store seasonal items, like sweaters and extra blankets for winter, that you're not ready to use in early fall. If your closet is big enough (and you don't have too many clothes to hang) you can also free up floor space by putting your dresser inside the closet. If you're lucky enough to be allowed to hang shelving, go for it. But you'll likely find that your hammer and nails are best left at home. Concrete walls are a big selling point for stocking up on mounting tape, self-adhesive hooks (the removable ones work great!), and sticky-back Velcro.

Thinking about furniture with multiple uses is also helpful. Your dresser can double as your TV stand. Bookshelves can store more than just books: frames, plants, and storage boxes can go here. Windowsills are also territory that shouldn't go unmarked (beware of sunlight-sensitive fabrics, CDs, and such).

Check your college Web site for prohibited items when it comes to lighting (candles are always a big no-no), heating (our Draft Snake on page 104 can make up for the no-space-heater-rule), and electrical equipment (toasters are considered a fire hazard). Fire safety is a big concern, so talk to your RA before starting any lighting projects (we have three oh-so-cool ones). And remember, we offer our one favorite look here. Take it as inspiration and apply your own twist. Search for the fabrics you can't live without, that make you happy, that say "you" all over. We've got the detailed instructions on how to make your dorm room fabulous, but it's up to you to make it your own.

What Color Says About You

Every successful design project starts with the right color. You want your dorm room to have a certain effect on you, your roommate, and your guests—and color can help you do that. What do you want to say about yourself in that room? Do you want to say "I just want to have fun!" or "I'm serious about my studies"? Either way, the right use of

BEFORE YOU DIAL . . .

Beyond the "where are you from?" inquiry, have these questions on hand when you call your new roommate for the first time. You'll make sure to coordinate with just one call (or e-mail) and cover all your bases.

When do you arrive? You want to plan how to divide the room together. You may also want to coordinate a lunch with your families.

What is your class schedule? You'll want to know when you'll have some private time in the room or whether you'll be getting up early too when her alarm goes off.

Do you plan to join any clubs? Try to find some common interests.

What is your sleep pattern? If it's different from yours, you can plan to work out lighting issues or some kind of bed separation, like a curtain panel. Check out our eyeshade on page 43.

What color is your bedding? Try to coordinate. You don't need the same color, but a nice complement in the same color family will make your room look more cohesive and less distracting.

Are you bringing a mini-refrigerator, extra seating, TV, DVD player, rug, floor lamp, iron and ironing board, microwave, or any other large items? Can we share?

What is your decorating style? If it's different from yours, you can try to coordinate by bringing in some elements you do like from that style, working together on a color scheme or choosing simpler patterns and solid prints.

Will you have a car? You may want to do some shopping together for room items; it's a good way to bond.

Have you seen the rooms? You may want to get her perspective on how it could work for both of you.

Is there anything else I should know about you? Does she have a boyfriend (he may be coming around a lot)? What are her daily habits and routines? Your schools can make sure not to put you with someone who smokes, but other issues may arise.

color can help you say it quietly, loudly, or somewhere in between.

We all have an emotional response to colors, even if we don't realize it. Some of us crave the richness of warm colors, like oranges and reds, while others savor the soothing cool of blues and greens. When deciding on a color scheme for your room, it's a good idea to talk to your roommate first. If she likes orange and you like blue, don't fret. You can still work together with these tips. It's all about finding the right hue that works for you.

To start, think about what you'll be doing in your room: You'll be primarily sleeping (cool, soft colors help you sleep best), but you'll also be studying (you might want something more stimulating in that area) and entertaining (something joyous and exuberant can keep the fête fun). Think about the light that comes into the room, too. Do you want light and cheery, or dark and moody? Your colors should reflect this.

When choosing color pairs, make sure to put them next to each other to determine whether they make a match. Colors respond to other colors in different ways, and to varied lighting. A red next to a pink could look orange, for example, depending on the pigment.

YOU AND HUE

There is no rule about how you will react to color; we all have different histories and cultures that force us to see a color differently. In general, though, these colors will yield a certain response from people.

Green: This earthy color is the universal symbol of nature. It's a good color for people in transition (that's you!). It promotes relaxation and renewal as well as purpose, order, and security. Girls who go for green are cheerful, lively, and friendly, but also a bit fickle.

Yellow: In small amounts, this bright and happy hue stimulates the intellect and awakens your creativity. It also speeds metabolism! A whole room in yellow, however, can have negative effects; it actually makes babies cry more, and the elderly anxious. Girls with a yen for yellow are intellectual, idealist, and have sunny dispositions, though they can be overly cautious.

Blue: This tranquil, calming color attracts the introspective and the educated. Brighter, richer blues, however, can increase energy. Girls who are true to blue are responsible, trustworthy, and compassionate, if a bit puritanical.

Red: Most people have a strong reaction to red: It's known to increase pulse rate, breathing, and even blood pressure. It's the color used in many restaurants because it makes you hungry by increasing your metabolism. Girls who love red, love life— they're ambitious, passionate, and outspoken.

Orange: Not everyone loves orange, which is surprising since it represents cheerfulness, well-being, intellect, and cooperation. Girls who are drawn to orange are confident, creative, and fun loving. They have adventurous streaks, too.

Purple: Most men, surprisingly, dislike this royal hue (maybe you should leave the grape-colored jacket at home on date night). But the girl who loves it is intelligent, sophisticated, and inspiring.

You'll find that we designated a color range to each chapter. Our bedroom area is draped in shades of blue; our study is in green; the wardrobe section is in the pink family; and you'll hang out in a juicy orange area. This is on purpose— not only to make sure the projects work together, but also because these colors inspired certain feelings. We'd love nothing more than to entertain our friends with a color that promotes cheerfulness, adventure, and cooperation!

The Setup

When you walk into your dorm room for the first time, you'll find your standard pieces of furniture: a bed, desk, chair, and dresser. Ditto for your roommate. They'll usually be arranged in the way the last roommates left them, but that doesn't mean you have to settle for that configuration.

Dorm rooms can come in any of a number of sizes and furniture plans. But we've come up with four solid layouts that work for most spaces. Remember: discuss with your roommate what you want to do, make sure you come up with a plan that works best for both of you, and have fun with it!

Your beds will be the most prominent pieces of furniture in your room. Start with positioning the two beds and fit everything else around them—or under them. Use as much wall space as you can to keep the center area open for moving and entertaining. Let's start.

Symmetrical

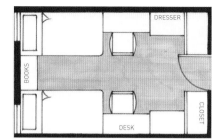

The benefit of this symmetrical plan, where the left side of the room mirrors the right, is its fabulous use of feng shui. Nothing blocks the path to the door (keeping your chi flowing in and out) and there is no obstruction in front of the window. In fact, you both get the use of a window, which is not only healthy for your well-being (you'll need that vitamin D and fresh air during long study hours), but the sill can also provide some much-needed storage space for books, plants, and family photos. Imagine that you and your roommate have stuck a piece of tape down the middle of the room and created your own defined spaces. This clean, straightforward floor plan gives you the feeling of two completely separate rooms, which helps with privacy (you're not climbing over each other to get to your belongings).

To pair any of these hues together, you want to follow one of the seven color harmonies of design. Remember the color wheel from art class? All colors derive from three primary colors: red, yellow, and blue. The warm colors fall on the right side of the wheel, while cool colors are on the left. The color directly opposite on the wheel is a color's complement. You can use black (the lack of color) and white (the entire spectrum of color) with any of these harmonies, and any value of color (light to dark), but you don't want to stray from these general rules of design.

Monochromatic: Choose one hue, such as red, in infinite values.

Complementary: Choose two hues, such as blue (cool) and orange (warm), from the opposite sides of the wheel to create high contrast.

Analogous: Choose three hues that are adjacent on the color wheel; for example, yellow, yellow-orange, and orange.

Split complement: Use one color and the two colors directly to the right and left of its complement, making an isosceles triangle on the wheel.

Triad: Choose colors that make an equilateral triangle on the color wheel.

Tetrad: Choose four colors that make a square or rectangle on the color wheel.

Hexad: Use all the colors in the wheel!

QUICK QUIZ! Look through design and fashion magazines—a great source of inspiration for your room—and determine what harmony a room that you love uses. This can help you determine what to look for when heading to the fabric store.

L-Shaped

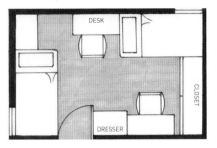

Putting your beds in an L-shape along the walls opens up the center of the room, making the most of wall space. It also provides a division between your bed and your roommate's bed: You won't be facing each other when you lie in bed. This plan provides a bit more visual interest than the symmetrical plan, making your room seem less boring. You could put the beds head to head, but you probably want some air space (snoring safeguard) by breaking up the beds with a desk. Again, if you can, try to find some window real estate for each of you. For both symmetrical and L-shaped plans, cement blocks offer valuable storage opportunities.

Bunked

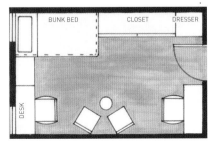

We love the bunk if you can both agree on who sleeps on the top and who sleeps on the bottom (there are benefits to either: low means not having to climb up to bed after party nights, while high means not having to sleep below any canoodling going on up above). We recommend this configuration because it offers up so much extra space, but it works only if your dorm's beds are bunk-compatible. You may even have enough room for an entertaining area (to fit a Better Bean Bag, see page 100). Try to keep the bunk beds by a window so you both get the benefit of sunlight.

Loft

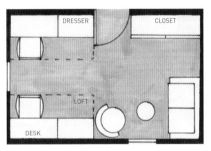

If you have a handyman (or woman) who can help you build a loft—and you don't mind spending a little extra cash to purchase the lumber—you'll find that you have a whole other room down below. You can fit a desk, sometimes a dresser, underneath, freeing up half your space for, say, a loveseat. (Who knows when the roommate will be out of town!) Check first that your school allows you to build a loft in the dorm, and ask your roommate if a) she minds and b) she'd like to partake in this great space-saver. Look for loft kits online, or loft builders posting ads on campus bulletin boards.

Don't Get Hung Up on Poster Art

Dorm room walls beg for your creative wisdom. Cement blocks are your blank canvases, and poster art your medium of choice. Nailing is most often a no-no, and actual paint is never an option. So, if posters it is, we came up with a few ideas to make your college art look, well, less like college art.

‣ Create a canvas: Give your poster art the museum treatment. All you need is mounting squares, a glue gun, a ready-made canvas, and four balsa wood pieces that cover the width and length of your canvas sides. Your poster should measure the same as the canvas. Mount the artwork on your canvas. Glue balsa wood pieces to their respective sides, ensuring that the ends overlap. Hang on mountable hooks.

‣ Slice 'em up: Using a craft knife, ruler, and craft cutting board, slice up one large print in quarters. Make sure you purchase four wood frames that will each fit one quarter. Paint the frames a monochromatic color that suits the whole image, and mount all four on the wall side by side in a grouping.

▸ Hang an artline: Inspired by the clothesline, use a length of craft wire (found at your local craft store) and tie one suction cup (also found at craft stores) at each end. Small binder clips, purchased or painted in colorful hues, act as clothespins. This works well for postcard-size prints or photos of family and friends.

▸ Make a DIY frame: Use ribbon or lace to frame your print. Measure your poster on all sides and add 4"; this is your ribbon yardage. Find a ribbon that enhances your print. It helps to find a secondary color in the print and match that with a solid or print ribbon. For bright, busy prints, we recommend a solid. For subtle prints, add more panache with a printed ribbon. You'll want to miter the corners of the ribbon for a more professional look; simply stitch a diagonal seam at the corners to create a 90 degree angle. Mount the poster to the wall first, and then frame with ribbon using a strip of mountable tape or self-adhesive Velcro.

▸ Decoupage a collage: First mount your poster onto a canvas board of the same size. Following the manufacturer's instructions, decoupage fabric scraps (stitch them first so they look sewn on for a cool effect), graphic food labels, or magazine clippings for an abstract piece.

▸ Revive with patchwork: Take two prints you no longer love and cut them into small bits. Rearrange them onto a piece of paper and copy on a high-quality color printer for a whole new print!

▸ Create a graffiti wall: Cut a long piece from a roll of white paper (found at a mailing center or craft shop) and mount it on a wall. Using self-adhesive Velcro, attach a range of colorful markers to the wall. You and your roommate can designate this area for writing memorable quotes from the year, or let visitors write whatever they please.

▸ Change it up: Use self-adhesive Velcro or removable stickymounts to mount your frames to the wall. This way you can replace prints whenever the mood strikes you.

The Perfect Arrangement

With high ceilings and box-shaped rooms, you usually have a lot of ground to cover when it comes to dorm walls. But you can designate areas of interest without making it look like a mess of Monets and Manets. You'll find that often anything goes when it comes to dorm room walls. The general rules can be broken, but you can create calm among the chaos of college art with a few helpful tips.

▸ Prep your prints: For arranging smaller prints, you can use paper the size of your posters to see how the arrangement will work on your wall. Tape them up and play with positioning. Once you've decided on a layout, mark the bottom edges and line up the real prints to mount.

▸ Start small: If you feel overwhelmed by all the white space, break up the wall visually and create several areas of interest. Place a large print in the center and arrange secondary prints around it in a radial pattern, or make a grid-like pattern of 8 x 10s toward one side of the wall and work your way over with other grouping types.

▸ Create balance: Dorm walls can desperately need full coverage, but placing prints at eye level (about 58" from the floor) is recommended. Try to create balance by arranging prints in groups: a random cluster of coordinating prints in one section; an uneven-numbered grouping of same-sized prints; or a linear pattern across the wall with multi-sized prints centered along the horizon.

▸ Think inner space: You want the prints of a group to be approximately 4" to 6" apart. This works well when you're putting together a large grouping of varying print sizes.

▸ Find symmetry: Always consider furniture when posting artwork. You want to frame your furniture with the artwork. Consider the dimensions above the furniture, and use that space to create a visually appealing display. For example, a 5" x 7" frame above a dresser just looks odd. Cover up that white space by working within the width of the dresser. Consider height, too. Shoot for a third of the dresser's height for visual balance.

Tools and Tricks

We know you've got plenty to ponder those first few months at school, so this handy reference is here when you need it. Refer back to this section when you have a question. Think of it as your own personal tech support. (Again, bolded words are defined in the glossary at the back of the book.)

Skill Level

Here's our rating system for how difficult you can expect a project to be. *Note:* they're listed right after the shopping list in each instruction.

101 - Freshman
An easy A.

201 - Sophomore
A bigger challenge, but still easy.

301 - Junior
A cinch if you have the time.

401 - Senior
Involved, but totally worth it.

Sewing Basics

Our number-one rule is to make sure you prewash and press all fabric before starting any project. (See page 124 for our Fabric Care Guide.)

Rather than repeat ourselves, we thought we'd give you a general supply list for all the sewing projects. If you come across a project you'd love to make and it says "Stitch Kit" in the supply list, head back here. Below is a list of what you will probably need. In fact, we recommend having these supplies on hand for any sewing project, like stitching loose buttons or mending a hem. Store them in a vintage box, a shoebox, a tackle box, or even a zip-top bag.

Stitch Kit

Fabric chalk or air-soluble marking pen
Hand-sewing needles
Press cloth
Scissors (for both paper and fabric)
Seam ripper
Straight pins and a pincushion
Tape measure and ruler
Thread

Choosing Thread

Cotton, rayon, machine quilting, metallic—choosing the right type of thread for your project isn't quite as simple as picking the right color. Using the wrong thread can damage your project and even your machine, so refer to this list when making your selection:

All-purpose: This strong thread is usually a polyester and cotton mix. It will hold up to most projects and be kind to your machine when working with light- to mid-weight fabrics.

Buttonhole and craft: Keep these reserved for just that—buttonholes and craft projects—and use all-purpose thread in your **bobbin**. These threads are heavier and will cause traditional seams to pucker or rip.

Extra-fine: This lightweight thread should only be used for sheer to very lightweight fabrics (like chiffon).

Heavyweight or upholstery: Use these threads as your top thread only and with a needle that has a larger eye. Load your bobbin with all-purpose thread.

Metallic: Metallic threads actually contain metal in them, so keep them away from your iron. Use needles

designated specifically for metallic threads to prevent shredding and reserve them for decorative stitching. Consult your manual for information on replacing a needle.

Rayon: This shiny thread is usually used for decorative stitching and machine embroidery. It's not strong enough to hold together traditional seams, so reserve it for those fancy touches.

Quilting: This thread is tailor-made for sewing and comes in hand-sewing or machine-sewing weight. They are both 100% cotton, but don't try to use the hand-sewing thread in the machine or you'll end up with a jammed bobbin.

TIP: If you can't match your thread to your project exactly, go for a color that is a shade darker than your fabric. Lighter colors will stand out more.

Choosing a Needle

As with thread, you need to match your needle to your project or you will end up with frayed thread, puckered seams, or broken needles.

Needles are sold in numbered sizes: the higher the number, the larger the needle. Because there are different measuring systems, machine needles come in a two-numbered system. The first number is the diameter of the needle in hundredths of millimeters, and the second number is the U.S. standard size.

Needles also come in a variety of types. Don't worry—you won't be tested later. Just keep the following page handy when you're going shopping.

Machine Needle Sizes	
Silky	60/8
Lightweight	70/10
Medium-weight	80/12
Medium- to heavyweight	90/14
Heavyweight	100/16
Upholstery	110/1

Needle Types

Ballpoint: These have a ball at the point of the needle to prevent causing snags. They're great for sewing knits.

Denim: These are stronger than universal needles, with a very sharp tip—perfect for heavier fabrics like denim and canvas.

Leather: These needles have wedge-shaped points, which help them slide in and out of layers of leather and suede.

Quilting: These needles are stronger and tapered to help them sew through the several layers of a quilt.

Sharp-point: These guys are thinner and sharper than universal needles, making them perfect for finer cottons.

Topstitching: These needles have a larger eye to accommodate the thicker topstitching decorative threads.

Universal point: These are great for most of your projects (and can do the job of every project in the book). Their tips are sharp, but slightly rounded.

Cutting

Craft knife: This won't work on fabric, but it's great for paper, cardstock, foam core, and cardboard. Here's how to use:

Always use a craft cutting board to avoid cutting into the surface below. Make sure to place the board over a flat surface (don't do this on your bed with the board on your lap—you could injure yourself!).

When starting any project, make sure the blade in your craft knife is new and sharp. You want a clean edge on your pieces; ragged edges will make a raggedy project.

A flat-edge metal ruler works best. The craft knife will glide along and not run over or into the ruler.

Press the ruler against the mark line, keeping fingers out of the blade's path.

If you're cutting foam core, run the blade along the mark line several times in one direction. It can take several slices before you cut through the foam. Don't tear pieces off; make sure the blade does the cutting.

Pinking shears: These look like regular scissors, but with zigzag blades. They cut a zigzag into the fabric to help prevent raveling. They work great for finishing the seam without having to sew the raw edge.

Rotary cutter: These guys are like pizza cutters for fabric. They're great for cutting out things fast, but always use a cutting board and a clear plastic sewing ruler (NOT a metal one).

Scissors: Keep a pair (or two if you can) around for cutting paper, cardstock, and the like. If you're dealing with fabric, embroidery floss, or anything else sewing-related, have a second pair designated for this only. Paper will dull scissors quickly and you'll never be able to use that pair on fabric again. It's always a good idea to have the handles of these scissors in different colors so you don't mix up the two (or use a permanent marker to write FABRIC ONLY and PAPER ONLY on them).

Marking Fabric

There are different marking tools you can use on fabric (to mark seam lines, darts, etc.). Here's how to get them on and off your projects.

Air-soluble marker: The marks will literally disappear on their own in a day or so. So if you're starting a project that you don't think you'll finish soon, try something else, or put your project in a zip-top bag and push out all the air.

Carbon paper: To use, lay this stuff facedown onto the **Wrong** side of your fabric (or paper) and put your template on top of it faceup. You can use a pencil or a tracing wheel to transfer your design onto your fabric.

The marks wash out in the washing machine, but it's a little harder to get rid of without washing it.

Permanent marker: These are permanent. No surprise here. Better to use them on the Wrong side only.

Tailor's or fabric chalk: This usually brushes off, or will come off with a damp cloth. It also comes out with dry cleaning if you want to get super-fancy.

Water-soluble marker: Washes right out with a few drops of water, so feel free to use on any fabrics that can be put in water (this means a big NO to some silks and draperies, so spot-check first!).

Adhesives (No Sew!)

There are adhesives you can use that work just as well as sewing. Here's how to sort through some of the stickiness.

Epoxy: This is usually a two-part glue that needs to be mixed together. It can come in a double-sided syringe-type packaging, or two separate bottles. This stuff will hold all sorts of things together, including metal to metal. It's really strong and usually quick to set. It's also hard to get off your skin and will damage your clothes, so wear an apron and be cautious when using. (Always defer to packaging instructions.)

Fabric glue: There are several types of fabric glues. Always do a spot-test on your fabric to make sure the glue won't be visible from the Right side when dry. Keep the motto "less is more" in mind when working with these; they are strong enough with just a small amount, and you don't want to ruin your fabric. They're also washable so they can act like stitches.

Fusible tapes: These are tapes that act like iron-on double-sided tape. They usually have a paper backing to protect your iron, and are great for hemming curtains and clothing quickly.

Gorilla Glue: Useful on most materials except fabric. It will even bond wood to plastic or metal. It can get messy and it's hard to get off of your hands, so it's not recommended for delicate work.

Hot-glue gun: These are now available in low temperature versions (that is, if you like keeping your fingerprints intact). They're perfect for many decorative crafty jobs like gluing trims to lampshades or frames, but will peel off most plastic surfaces.

Rubber cement: This comes in a can or bottle, and brushes on. Use in a well-ventilated area or you'll end up with a headache. This works well for sticking something to a flat surface.

Spray adhesive: This comes in temporary and permanent varieties. It works well for sticking paper or fabric to large surfaces, like lampshades, bulletin boards, or foam core. The temporary stuff works well to hold together layers of fabric (especially when working with batting).

Super Glue: This stuff holds things together like Superman, but it's also super-hard to get off. Start out with small amounts. It's great for slick things like plastic, glass, and metal, but it doesn't work as well on porous surfaces like wood or fabric.

White craft-glue: This is the glue you'll recognize from elementary school. It's water-soluble and nontoxic, so it's a pretty safe bet all around.

Standard Machine Stitches

The most useful tool when troubleshooting problems with your machine will be your machine's manual, so don't lose it! If you've found your machine at a thrift store or been given a hand-me-down, call the manufacturer. They can usually supply you with a manual for a small price.

Practically every machine these days has the two stitches that you will use in this book: a straight and a zigzag. You may vary the length and width of the stitches, but really those two are all you need. From these two stitches you will be able to do all of the following (amazing, we know):

Stitches

Backstitch: This is sewing backward. Your machine will have either a button or a lever to pull to make the machine sew in reverse. Usually this will have a symbol on it that looks like a U-turn symbol. Backstitching a couple of stitches when you start and stop a stitch will help secure the thread in place, sort of like a knot.

Basting stitch: Basting is typically used for temporary stitches (for when you need to hold fabric in place), to be removed later. To baste, set your machine to a long straight stitch (typically 5 to 6 mm) and sew as usual. Their longer length makes them easier to pick out.

Edgestitch: This is a straight stitch close to an edge, which is helpful when sewing on trims or securing multiple layers of fabric together around the edges.

Satin stitch: This is a wide, short zigzag stitch and looks great on appliqués. Set your machine to a zigzag stitch and attach the proper **presser foot** to avoid broken needles. Adjust the machine settings to about 60 stitches per inch. You can adjust the width and length to your liking. If you see puckering, try putting a piece of tear-away stabilizer behind the fabric.

Straight stitch: A traditional straight stitch will usually be the default on your machine. It's typically 3 mm long, but it doesn't have to be. Experiment to get the look you want.

Topstitch: A topstitch is a visible straight stitch sewn on the Right side (or top!) of the project. You can use a thicker thread or contrasting color to make the stitching more visible. (For an example, check out the Fleece Robe on page 118.)

Making Seams

When sewing a seam, be sure to keep your **seam allowance** in mind: That's the distance between the needle and the raw edge. The markings on your machine have been set to be correct when your needle is in the center position, so you may need to adjust your needle position where necessary.

We've used these two seams in the book:

Traditional Seam: To make this seam, pin your fabric with the Right sides facing and the raw edges even. Machine-sew using the seam allowance that was indicated in your instructions or pattern.

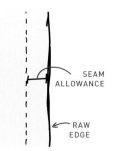

SEAM ALLOWANCE

RAW EDGE

Flat-fell seam: This creates a strong seam without any raw edges. To start, pin your fabrics together with the Right sides facing and the raw edges even, like a traditional seam. Sew the seam using the seam allowance allotted. Trim one side of the seam allowance down to ⅛", then press it toward the trimmed side (step 1). Fold the wider seam allowance piece around the shorter one, wrapping the wider side's raw edge behind the trimmed side (step 2). Press and pin the seam in place. Sew again close to the folded edge to create the second line of stitching (step 3).

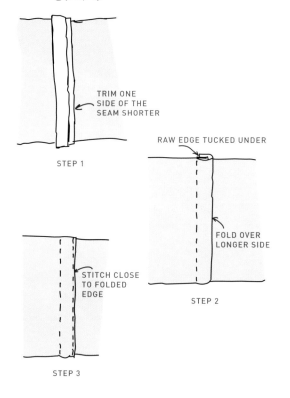

TRIM ONE SIDE OF THE SEAM SHORTER

STEP 1

RAW EDGE TUCKED UNDER

FOLD OVER LONGER SIDE

STEP 2

STITCH CLOSE TO FOLDED EDGE

STEP 3

Sewing and Clipping Corners

When you're sewing a corner, there are two things you should remember: pivoting and clipping. When you sew up to a corner, leave your needle piercing the fabric, lift the presser foot, and turn the fabric 90 degrees to make the corner. Lower the presser foot again and sew in the new direction to pivot. Once you've sewn the corner, you'll need to clip away the seam allowance as shown for it to turn to the Right side bulk-free.

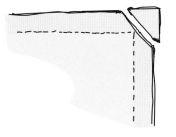

Hand Sewing

We won't have you sewing much by hand for these projects. All you'll need to know are these two stitches:

Running stitch: This is the most basic (and oldest) of all the sewing stitches.

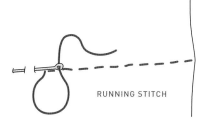

RUNNING STITCH

You can sew it tightly for a seam or do it loosely for a basting stitch. Try to make the stitches as even as possible by weaving the needle in and out of the fabric.

Slipstitch: This stitch is invisible and works well for sewing invisible **hems** or sewing things shut, like pillows or pouches. To sew a pillow opening closed, you'll be slipping the needle into the fold on either side as you sew. If you're hemming, just slip the needle into the hem and then take it onto the Right side of the fabric as shown.

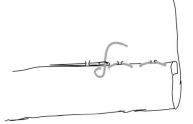

SLIPSTITCH

Embroidery

Embroidery is a great craft that you can take along with you to work on between classes or on a road trip with friends. Here are a few tips to help get you started:

Get an embroidery hoop. It stabilizes the fabric as you stitch, making your job much easier. While you're hooping, be sure not to stretch the fabric too much so you won't warp the design.

Try embroidering with various numbers of threads and even yarns. If it can pass through the fabric without shredding, you can embroider with it.

If you're going to embroider a knit (like a T-shirt), you'll need to put some stabilizer behind it so that the fabric doesn't warp while you're stitching it.

Here are all the basic stitches you'll need:

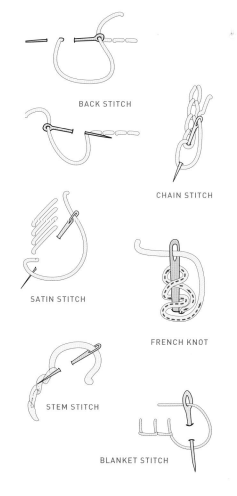

BACK STITCH

CHAIN STITCH

SATIN STITCH

FRENCH KNOT

STEM STITCH

BLANKET STITCH

Choosing Fabrics and Trims

Fabric shops are like ice cream shops. You walk in and every flavor of material is there for the picking. While rows upon rows of fabric bolts can provide endless inspiration, they can also be a bit intimidating if you're new to sewing. We'll help sort through the lingo and labels so you can determine what will work best for your project. While not all projects in this book are sewn, it's a good idea to know the characteristics of fabric and trims when embarking on any craft project: Will it wash well? How do I iron it? Could I use it on a pillow? These are smart lessons you'll take with you to college and beyond.

Fabrics 101

Fabrics are typically sold by the yard off of bolts. You'll want to take a close look at the labels on these bolts to learn the name of the fabric (in case you need to come back for more), care instructions (so you know if you can wash it easily), pattern **repeat** (for larger projects; this matters when determining yardage), and pricing (usually by the yard). Always prewash and press fabrics before embarking on a project. See the Fabric Care Guide

on page 124 for details on fabrics that need prewashing.

If you're new to sewing, stick with fabrics like cotton that don't have any stretch or slip—knits and slippery fabrics will be more difficult to sew. We use mostly cottons and felts in this book because they are so easy to handle. If you've fallen hopelessly in love with the print of a stretchy fabric, try incorporating it into an easier, smaller project so you can get the hang of it (like the eyeshade project on page 43).

For embellishments or anything you're simply going to glue, you have more flexibility in choosing a material. Just make sure to do a spot-test on your fabric and trim before you apply fabric glue, which may leave a stain on the finished side.

Also, check the hand (or feel) of your fabric to make sure it will be a good candidate for your project. If you're making a duvet cover or a pillow, you don't want something that's going to be itchy or irritating.

Before you hit the fabric store, narrow your efforts (and budget) with these handy tips:

- Make a shopping list. You don't want to risk forgetting one small item and not being able to start on your project

- Bring swatches of fabrics you want to match. Don't trust your memory. You may get home and find that the green was more kelly than lime.

- Be flexible. You may have your heart set on a certain color or style, but chances are the store won't have exactly what you have in mind. Go with a general idea of what you like and keep your options open for a more enjoyable experience.

- Stay within budget. If a high-priced fabric catches your eye, see if you can make up the difference by choosing cheaper trims. Just watch your limits as you shop. Don't grab things blindly and get sticker shock at the counter.

Nap time

Some fabrics have a **nap**: a texture that runs in one direction. These fabrics include fur (faux and real), velvet, corduroy, velour, and suede. The nap causes the fabric to look different from different angles. If you can run your hand down the length of the fabric and affect the way it looks (you're pushing the nap up and down), then you need to keep a few things in mind while you're working:

- Run your hand over the fabric so that it feels smooth (the nap is facing downward). Always lay your pattern pieces running in the same direction. For example, on the Fuzzy Slippers on page 116, if you cut out one foot with the fur running from toe to heel, you should cut the other piece in the same direction.

- It's usually easiest to lay your pattern pieces on the Wrong side of the fabric, trace them with a fabric-marking tool, and then cut them out.

- If you're using fur or shearling, cut through one layer at a time. You may think you're saving time by folding it in half and cutting, but trust us; you'll damage the fur. When you are cutting, you should only cut through the back layer, *without* cutting through the fur on the Right side. Make small snips to avoid a big fuzzy mess, and to keep the fur clean and intact on the Right side. After you sew your pieces together, you can use a straight pin to pull out any fur that gets caught in the seams.

Velvet, Meet Vinyl

Got your eye on more than one fabric type, you two-timer? Don't worry; we've been there. When working with two types of fabrics, first check that you can handle and wash them both the same way. You don't want to sew together a dry-clean-only fabric with a washable one and then have to dig deep for dry-cleaning dollars every time you spill coffee on it. This goes for trims, too. Wash them before using them on any project that you will wash. Color-bleeding on a handmade project can be devastating.

All the Trimmings

Trims are the best way to adorn your projects, make them look finished, and add a more personalized look. Adding a trim is as easy as hot-gluing your favorite find along the edge of a lampshade or adding a bit of piping in the seam of just about any decor project.

Bias Tape: Bias tape is sold in a wide variety of colors and widths, by the package or by the yard. Single-fold bias tape has been folded in half once and has a Wrong side. Double-fold bias tape (used on the Desktop Catchall [page 80], for example) has been folded in half twice and does not have a Wrong side.

To make your own single-fold bias tape (this can be fun if you want to use a print), determine the width of the finished tape you want and double that measurement. For example, if you want a ½" wide single-fold tape, you'll need to cut a strip of fabric along the bias (45 degrees from the selvage) that is 1" wide. Using an iron, press each long raw edge toward the center on the Wrong side.

To make your own double-fold bias tape, determine the width of the finished tape you want and multiply it by four. For example, if you want a ½" wide finished double-fold tape, you'll need to cut a strip of fabric along the bias that is 2" wide. After you cut your bias strip, use the iron to press each long raw edge toward the center on the Wrong side, just like you did for the single fold. To create the double fold, press the tape in half again, enclosing the raw edges.

Cording and piping: Some people use these terms interchangeably, but usually piping is a strip of bias-cut fabric that has been sewn around a cotton cord or rope, and cording is a braided trim often with a lip (or flange). Keep in mind that usually it's that lip that goes inside a seam to be sewn. Cording without a lip can usually be hand-sewn or glued.

Gimp: No, we're not talking about *Pulp Fiction*. Gimp is actually a trim that is used to hide seams in home decor projects. It's slightly heavy, and has a decorative loopy weave to it.

Ribbon: Ribbon can come in just about as many varieties as fabric, including picot (the kind with the little nubs along the sides), grosgrain (which has horizontal grooves in it), velvet, satin (double or single-sided), taffeta, silk, wired, sheer, and embroidered.

Rickrack: Rickrack is trim that looks like a long zigzag and comes in many widths and colors. You may recognize it from your clothing as a kid, but it almost always adds a quirky charm to whatever project you're working on (like the Reversible Duvet Cover on page 24).

Specialty trims: Beaded or sequined, fringed or flowered, these elegant embellishments can add sparkle and charm to just about anything.

WHERE YOU SLEEP

Tired of your standard bed-in-a-bag? Make your bedding all your own with lively prints and cheeky pillows that won't make you snore. Soft blues and dreamy teals (with a splash of black and white) soothe you to sleep—so you'll be fresh (OK, awake) for that 8:00 A.M. class.

Reversible Duvet Cover

It's perfectly fine to be fickle when it comes to style. One day you want white, the other you want black. (Incidentally, the day you want black may just happen to arrive the day after you spill coffee on the white.) This twin-sized duvet cover gives you the choice of both so you never get bored. On one side, a romantic damask-inspired print looks fresh and modern with playful pom-poms; on the other, solid black with a border of white rickrack shows off your mysterious side.

Cut the fabric.

1 From the damask, cut:
1 front: 32" wide x 90" long (make sure it has an even **repeat** down the center)

Stitch the trim.

2 Turn the damask **Wrong**-side up and iron a 1" fold along each long side.

3 Pin, then stitch the pom-pom trim along each long side of the damask. It's easier if you use a **cording foot** on your machine for this step.

4 Turn the damask **Right**-side up and center it on the Right side of the white sheet. Trim any extra sheet fabric that extends beyond the damask's top and bottom.

5 Pin, then stitch the fabric to the sheet. Use a cording foot and be careful not to sew over the pom-poms.

continued

P.S. In the 12th century, damask was named after the city of Damascus. This ancient city is famous for its textiles, and it was here that weavers perfected this ornamental print.

YOU'LL NEED:

- 2½ yards (45" wide) damask print in cotton
- 5 yards black pom-pom trim
- 9¼ yards medium rickrack in black
- 6½ yards medium rickrack in white
- 1 flat twin-sized sheet in black
- 1 flat twin-sized sheet in white
- 6 self-adhesive Velcro squares
- Yardstick or measuring tape
- Sewing machine
- **Cording foot** for the machine (optional)
- Iron and ironing board
- Stitch Kit (see page 14)

SKILL LEVEL

6 Pin, then stitch a layer of black rickrack 5" from the pom-poms along both sides. (A straight stitch works fine on rickrack.)

7 Pin, then stitch another layer of black rickrack 2" from the first layer, on both sides.

Embellish the reverse side.

8 Place the white sheet over the black sheet. Trim any excess black fabric that extends beyond the top and bottom of the white sheet. Put the white sheet aside.

9 Measure and mark 12" from the sides and 4" from the top and bottom of the black sheet.

10 Pin, then stitch a layer of white rickrack along the marked rectangle, **mitering** corners.

Make the duvet cover.

11 Place the white sheet over the black sheet, Right sides facing.

12 Twin-sized duvets are usually 64" wide by 86" long. Measure your sheet's final width and length and subtract 64 and 86 from those measurements, respectively. Divide the results in half. For example: if your sheet is 16" longer than your duvet, using your fabric pencil and yardstick, draw a line 8" from the sheet's top and another 8" from the sheet's bottom. Repeat for the width.

13 Pin along the marked lines, leaving the cover's bottom open.

14 Stitch the sheets together along the marked lines at the sides and top, remembering to leave the bottom unstitched. To keep the fabric from fraying, trim the raw edges with **pinking shears** 1" from the stitch line. If you don't have pinking shears, sew another line of stitches ½" from the edge to secure the seam.

15 Cut any excess fabric 3" above the bottom marking. Fold, then press under at the marked line. Stitch 1" from the fold around the bottom opening. Again, trim the raw edges with pinking shears. Turn the cover Right-side out.

16 Stick Velcro squares to the bottom opening's inside **hem** at the corners, at the rickrack layers, and at the pom-poms.

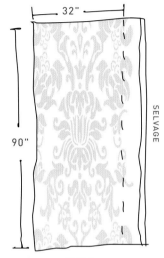

STEP 1

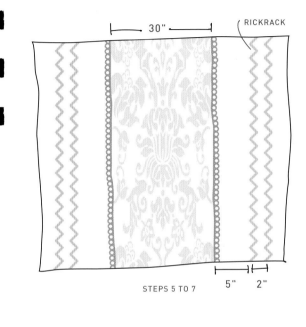

30"

RICKRACK

5" 2"

STEPS 5 TO 7

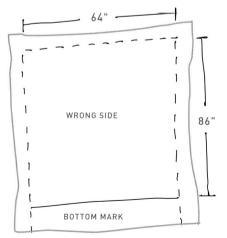

64"

WRONG SIDE

86"

BOTTOM MARK

STEP 12

LOW-SEW OPTION

1 twin-size duvet cover in white or black

2½ yards (45" wide) cotton damask print or print to match

5 yards pom-pom trim in black

9¼ yards medium rickrack in black

6½ yards medium rickrack in a coordinating color

Fabric glue

2½ yards fusible web

Stitch Kit (page 14)

1 Repeat steps 1 and 2 from the sew option. Duvet covers range from 83" to 86" in length. Measure the length of yours and use that number to fold and press the damask top and bottom under to match the length of the cover. Trim the folded-under edges to 1".

2 Repeat step 3 from the sew option. Secure the pom-poms's raw edges under with glue or by **tacking.**

3 Iron fusible web down over the damask's entire **Wrong** side, according to the manufacturer's instructions. Pin, then iron the damask to the center of the duvet cover, matching the top and bottom ends.

4 Glue or **hand-tack** every fifth pom-pom to secure.

5 Stitch the damask along the duvet cover's opening to secure it in place.

6 Repeat steps 6 and 7 from the sew option, folding and securing the rickrack under 1" at ends.

7 Repeat steps 9 and 10 from the sew option using the coordinating color on the reverse side.

Rainy Day Curtain

Dress your window for the weather: a cheerful umbrella **appliqué** for those gloomy days, and a crisp white panel for when the sun comes out. Your best bet for dorm windows is an adjustable tension rod (no brackets mean no drilling). Otherwise, a width of sticky-back Velcro at the top of this panel will keep peeping Toms peeping elsewhere.

Make the appliqué.

1 Iron fusible web to the **Wrong** side of the light blue cotton (enough to cover the umbrella top) and the Wrong side of the white cotton (enough to cover the umbrella top and handle). Iron fusible web to the Wrong side of the white and black polka-dot cotton (enough for 4 raindrops).

2 Trace the umbrella top template onto the Wrong sides of the light blue fabric and the white fabric. Trace the umbrella handle onto the Wrong side of the white fabric. Trace the raindrops onto the Wrong side of the white and black polka-dot fabric.

3 From the light blue cotton, cut:
1 umbrella top

From the white cotton, cut:
1 umbrella top
1 umbrella handle

From the white and black polka-dot cotton, cut:
4 raindrops

Cut the curtain panel.

4 Based on your window measurements, mark the length and width of your teal fabric (the rainy side) and your white fabric (the sunny side) and allow for a 1" **seam allowance** on all sides.

Stitch the appliqué.

5 Peel away the fusible web carefully from the white cotton pieces. Place and press the white umbrella on the **Right** side of the teal panel,

continued

YOU'LL NEED:

- Umbrella and raindrop templates
- ½ yard (45" wide) cotton fabric in light blue print
- ½ yard (45" wide) cotton fabric in white
- ¼ yard (45" wide) cotton fabric in white with black polka-dots
- Cotton fabric in teal and white polka-dot for the rainy panel (for yardage: see "How to Measure a Window," page 31)
- Cotton fabric in white for the plain panel (for yardage: see "How to Measure a Window," page 31)
- ½"-wide rickrack in black (for yardage: add length and width of the panel and multiply by two)
- 1 yard fusible web
- Yardstick or measuring tape
- Sewing machine
- Iron and ironing board
- Stitch Kit (see page 14)

approximately 4" diagonally from the bottom right corner, or as desired.

6 Use a **zigzag stitch** (see your machine manual) along the edges of the appliqué.

7 Repeat with the other pieces, as shown in the photo. Make sure the white umbrella peeks from behind the top of the blue umbrella top, as a shadow would. You can use a straight stitch on the raindrops.

Apply the rickrack.

8 On the white panel, pin, then stitch black rickrack in a rectangle: 4" from the left and right sides, 6" from the top, and 5" from the bottom. **Miter** at the corners.

Stitch the curtain.

9 With the Right sides facing, place the white panel over the teal panel. Mark a horizontal line 2" from the top, and another line 1½" below that line. Leave that part unstitched; this is your rod pocket. Use a yardstick to mark 1" from the side and top edges, leaving the bottom (where the appliqué is located) open. Pin at the mark lines and stitch, remembering to leave the rod pocket openings and the bottom unstitched.

10 Finish the edges with **pinking shears**, press the seams flat, and turn the curtain inside out.

Stitch the rod pocket.

11 Pin along both rod-pocket lines. Stitch along these lines, leaving the ends open. Make sure the top thread matches the front fabric and your **bobbin** thread matches the back side, and sew with the front of the curtain facing up as it goes through the sewing machine.

12 Fold and press the raw edge of the bottom fabric inside by 2". Then **top-stitch** a 1" **hem** along the bottom.

2"

1½"

UNSTITCHED

WRONG SIDE

OPEN

STEP 9

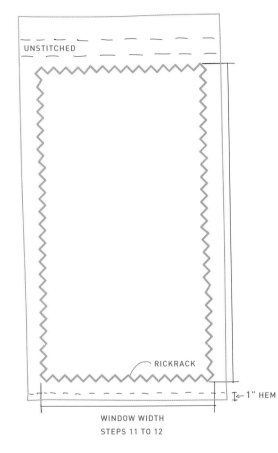

UNSTITCHED

RICKRACK

1" HEM

WINDOW WIDTH
STEPS 11 TO 12

HOW TO MEASURE A WINDOW

Your dorm window may be the first of many you'll measure for curtains. Here are a few quick and simple steps to ensure an accurate fit.

1. On your first visit to the dorm, bring a 16'- to 25'-long steel tape measure (the kind that stays stiff while you measure).

2. Draw a quick sketch of the window so that you can write down the proper measurements.

3. For most dorms, you'll hang the curtain inside the frame (an outside-frame mount requires drilling brackets into the wall). You want to measure the width inside the frame and the desired length. If you want to make floor-length curtains, measure from the top inside frame to the floor; otherwise, to the sill will do.

4. Most cotton fabrics are sold in 45" widths. You want your curtain to have a little fullness so it drapes nicely; we recommend 1½ times fullness. So, for windows that are 30" or less, you can use one panel (or one width of fabric). For windows wider than 30", you can either stitch two widths of fabric together to make one panel, or make two separate panels.

5. Your finished length determines your yardage; however, if you need more than one width of fabric (wider than 45"), your width counts too. To calculate yardage, you need to figure out the width plus half the width for fullness plus 2" for seams. For example, if your window is 24" wide, you would need 24" + 12" + 2" = 38" (you can use one width of fabric here, so simply purchase yardage based on your finished length). If you needed two widths of fabric, you'd double your length for yardage needed. For a finished length, add 2" to the measured length that you want (for a 1" top and bottom hem).

Cocoon Lampshade

Dorm room lighting leaves much to be desired as far as style. Overheads are harsh and you rarely get a dimmer function, so stock up on lamps that allow you to brighten or dim the room depending on what you're doing. This pendant lamp not only looks cool, but when you hang it from your ceiling or window, it's a space saver, too. Even better, it's a no-sew project.

Fit the fabric.

1 Hang the pendant shade and wrap felt around it, ensuring a close fit, a fully closed back (overlapping ends by approximately 2"), and a 1" fold at top (keeping a distance from a low-watt bulb). Pin the back closed.

Trace the templates.

2 Using chalk, trace all three templates onto the 1 yard felt (while on the pendant) as desired, leaving the bottom edge for later.

3 Trace the butterfly templates onto the white felt square and cut them out. Set aside.

Cut the fabric.

4 Unpin and remove the felt from the shade. Use embroidery scissors to trim around the butterfly wings (leaving the body uncut) and petals (leaving the area around the point uncut).

5 Replace the felt on the shade with the chalk side facing in. Use Velcro squares to close the back.

6 Place the felt templates from step 3 along the shade's bottom edge (these templates are easier than paper to manage when working without a hard surface). Trim around the bottom of the templates only, carefully keeping the full tops of the bodies attached. *Hint:* Place several templates in a row so edges transition seamlessly.

STEP 1

1"

YOU'LL NEED:

• Cocoon templates (small and large butterflies and petals)

• 1 pendant lamp, about 11" in diameter (for a larger pendant lamp, use more white felt)

• 1 yard (60" wide) white felt

• 1 white felt square

• Fabric chalk

• Embroidery scissors

• 4 self-adhesive Velcro squares

SKILL LEVEL 201

P.S. Go eco with compact fluorescent lightbulbs (CFLs) and feel good every time you flip the switch. They'll last longer, too.

BONUS PROJECT:
COCOON BARREL SHADE

Can't hang a ceiling light in your room? Here's a twist on the pendant shade that works great as a desk or bedside lamp.

1 From the felt, cut:
40 petals

2 Pair two petals together and place them on the shade as shown in the photo, four pairs stacked in a row. Rows should be approximately 4" apart.

3 Glue the petals to the shade. The felt may naturally stick to the shade, depending on the shade fabric; otherwise, use pins to hold the petals in place until the glue dries.

Note: For another great use of the cocoon templates, check out the Cozy Cocoon Pillow on page 50.

P.S. Felt is the oldest fabric known to man (and woman), and it's also the name of an '80s British alt-rock band. Who knew?

YOU'LL NEED:

- Cocoon template (petals only)
- 1 desk lamp with a barrel shade
- ¼ yard (60" wide) felt (for an 11"-diameter shade; use more felt for a larger shade) in a color that contrasts with the lampshade
- Fabric glue
- Small scissors
- Straight pins (optional)

SKILL LEVEL 101

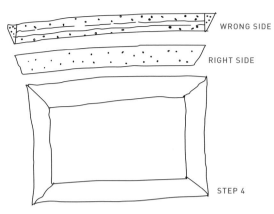

WRONG SIDE

RIGHT SIDE

STEP 4

Monogram Sham

Your initials are your ultimate personal statement—but sometimes one simple letter can make an even bigger impact. A little punctuation adds punch to this edgier version of the traditionally preppy monogram.

Cut the border fabric.

1 Measure the width and length of the sham's **flange** on all sides.

2 From the polka-dot fabric, cut:
2 side strips: the flange's width x 1" longer than the flange's sides
2 strips: the flange's width x 1" longer than the flange's top and bottom

Add the new border.

3 Fold and press over ½" on the long sides of one long strip.

4 Place the strip over the corresponding flange and **miter** the short ends to match the sham's corners. Trim ½" from the diagonal on the **Wrong** side.

5 Pin the polka-dot strip over the flange and stitch it in place.

6 Repeat steps 3 to 5 on the other sides.

7 Pin, then stitch rickrack to the inner rectangle, hiding the edge of the polka-dot fabric.

Make the monogram.

8 Draw a block letter of your first initial using a pencil and ruler, or print one in your favorite computer typeface (within a 16" x 16" area) to fit the front of the sham. It could be an elegant script or a bold sans-serif block letter— whatever you love. Cut out the letter. This will be your monogram template.

9 Place the monogram template **Right**-side down on the black felt. Trace the letter on the black felt with the chalk. Cut: 1 letter

10 Pin, then stitch the letter Wrong-side down to the sham's face. Add a 1½" diameter felt circle for the period, if desired.

YOU'LL NEED:

- One pillowcase sham
- ½ yard (45" wide) black fabric with white polka-dots
- 3¼ yard (½" wide) rickrack in black
- ½ yard (60" wide) black felt
- Pencil and ruler (or computer and printer)
- Sewing machine
- Iron and ironing board
- Stitch Kit (see page 14)

MORE MONOGRAMS:
DON'T LET THE BEDBUGS BITE!

Choosing cotton instead of felt for your monogram has some perks and quirks. You have the advantage of playing with fun patterns like the ladybug print here, but it's also a bit more involved because of fraying.

Print your letter.

1. Choose a letter in a typeface you like (we chose Mesquite Standard for the W and Script MT Bold for the D) and increase it approximately 800%. You'll need to print on 11" x 17" paper. Play with sizes to see what you prefer.

2. Cut out the letter. This is your monogram template.

Make the monogram.

3. Place the template over the desired area of the cotton solid.

4. Cut a square around the letter from the fabric and remove the template. Repeat steps 3 and 4 with the cotton print.

5. Press fusible web to the back of each fabric square, according to the manufacturer's instructions.

6. Put the monogram **Right**-side down on the fusible side of the solid fabric, and trace around it. Cut along the trace line.

7. Remove the fusible web carefully from the cotton solid, avoiding fraying at the ends. Place the letter on the center of the pillowcase or pillow. Press according to the fusible web's instructions.

Stitch the monogram.

8. If using a pillowcase: use a **zigzag stitch** along the edge of the letter (no-sew for pillow).

9. For either a pillow or a pillowcase: repeat step 6 with the cotton print. Place and press the letter over the solid letter, adjusting to create a shadow effect.

10. If using a pillowcase: repeat the zigzag stitch around this letter.

STITCH PRACTICE

If you're new to your machine, or have been stuck on the straight stitch for years, try this tip to experiment with different stitches. Take a scrap of solid-colored fabric (preferably cotton or felt) and, using contrasting thread, play around with width and foot settings, then stitch in a straight line. For each test stitch, write down the settings you used for future reference. Pin the sampler up on a bulletin board or near your machine so you can choose the right stitch for your project. Consult your machine's manual for available settings and stitch options.

YOU'LL NEED:

▸ Computer and printer
▸ ½ yard (45" wide) cotton solid
▸ ½ yard (45" wide) cotton print
▸ 1 yard fusible web
▸ Pillowcase or throw pillow
▸ Sewing machine (optional)
▸ Iron and ironing board
▸ Stitch Kit (see page 14)

Easy-Embellish Sheets

Matching sheets are a must for the budding dorm designer. For extra-long sheets a fun flap is the way to go, or you can turn up the style quotient with embroidery or appliqué. Let this project remind you that you don't have to splurge on expensive designer sheets—you can make them yourself!

Prepare the sheet.

1 Remove the end flap of the sheet, if one exists, using scissors or a seam ripper.

Cut the fabric.

2 Measure the sheet's width:
If it's wider than the width of your fabric, you'll need to cut two strips from the fabric and sew them together to match the sheet's width. Cut:
2 white polka-dot pieces: Each should be 11" long, and a width that is half the width of the sheet plus ¾".
If the sheet's width is smaller than the width of your fabric, cut:

1 white polka-dot piece: 11" in length by the width of the sheet plus 1".

3 If you cut one piece above, skip to the next step. If you cut two pieces, face the two short ends together, **Right** sides together, and stitch a ½" seam to create one long piece. Press the seam flat.

4 With the fabric Right-side down, fold and press a ½" seam along all edges. Fold and press the 11" length in half, **Wrong** sides together.

Stitch the fabric.

5 Pin the new flap to the top of your sheet, allowing the flap to hide the top sheet's raw edges by ½". Pin the short

ends as well, with the fabric folded inside. Stitch ¼" from the side edges and along the bottom of the flap.

Add the finishing touches.

6 Pin, then stitch a layer of rickrack along the stitch line where the sheet and flap meet (make sure your **bobbin** thread matches the sheet color). Fold 1" to the other side.

7 Cut two 1" diameter circles from the black felt and cover the rickrack ends on both sides by **hand-tacking** at the circle's center.

Low-sew option! Use fabric glue to adhere the rickrack and circles over the flap. It's washable and dries quickly.

YOU'LL NEED:

▸ One extra-long twin white flat sheet

▸ ¾ yard (45" wide) white fabric with black polka-dots

▸ 2 yards (½" wide) rickrack in light blue

▸ 1 black felt square

▸ Fabric glue (optional)

▸ Sewing machine

▸ Iron and ironing board

▸ Stitch Kit (see page 14)

YOU'LL NEED:

▸ Eyeshade template

▸ ¼ yard (45" wide) cotton print

▸ ¼ yard (45" wide) coordinating cotton print

▸ ½ yard (45" wide) elastic (preferably double-faced)

▸ Handful of Poly-fil or lavender

▸ Sewing machine

▸ Iron and ironing board

▸ Stitch Kit (see page 14)

SKILL LEVEL **101**

Hangover-Helper Eyeshade

Yes, we know how that freshman year can be. You're free to do exactly what you want, and sometimes that means a little excess in the cocktail department. Whether you're suffering from a late night of studying or socializing (or just want to get some Z's before your roommate hits the lights) this eyeshade is just the thing to block out the world.

Trace the template.

1 Using fabric chalk, trace the eyeshade template over the desired area on both prints, on the **Wrong**-side. From one cotton print, cutting ½" from the trace line, cut:

1 front

From the coordinating print, cutting ½" from the trace line, cut:

1 back

Pin the pieces in place.

2 Lay one piece of the fabric **Right**-side up. Place the elastic along the center width and pin one end to the left-hand side of the eyeshade, leaving 1" of elastic beyond the raw edge. Tuck the rest of the elastic inside the template area, pinning it flat (see diagram).

3 Face the Right sides of the fabrics together and pin.

Stitch the shade.

4 Machine- or handstitch along the trace line, leaving the right-hand side of the eyeshade open.

5 Press inside the seam line (this will make your eyeshade look better when it's done) and turn it Right-side out.

6 Fill the shade evenly with Poly-fil or lavender (don't overstuff), and pin it closed.

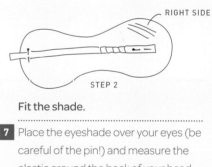

RIGHT SIDE

STEP 2

Fit the shade.

7 Place the eyeshade over your eyes (be careful of the pin!) and measure the elastic around the back of your head. Mark a comfortable point.

8 Place the loose end of the elastic inside the opening (temporarily removing the pin) and replace the pin at the mark.

9 **Slipstitch** the opening closed and get some sleep.

YOU'LL NEED:

- ¾ yard (54" wide) white faux fur
- ¾ yard (54" wide) animal print faux fur
- 1 pillow form (20" x 20")
- Sewing machine
- Stitch Kit (see page 14)

SKILL LEVEL 101

White and Wild Shag Pillow

White fur (even faux) can feel luxurious and sophisticated, very Marilyn Monroe. But we know, sometimes your penchant for animal print can roar. We went Arctic with pure white, but if it moves you, break out a wild zebra or bobcat print on one side of this reversible shag pillow.

Cut the fabric.

1. Cut through the back of the fabric, and not through the fur.
From the white fur, cut:
1 front: 21" x 21"

   From the animal print, cut:
1 back: 21" x 21"

Pin the pillow.

2. Using fabric chalk and ruler, mark a ½" seam around all sides on the back of one fur piece.

3. Face the **Right** sides of the front and back together and pin along the seam line, tucking the fur around the edges toward the center. You can trim any extra fur from the seam after sewing to eliminate bulk.

Stitch the pillow.

4. Stitch around all sides, leaving a 12" opening on one side.

5. Trim the corners on the diagonal before turning it Right-side out (again, to eliminate bulk). Stuff the pillow form into the opening and **slipstitch** it closed.

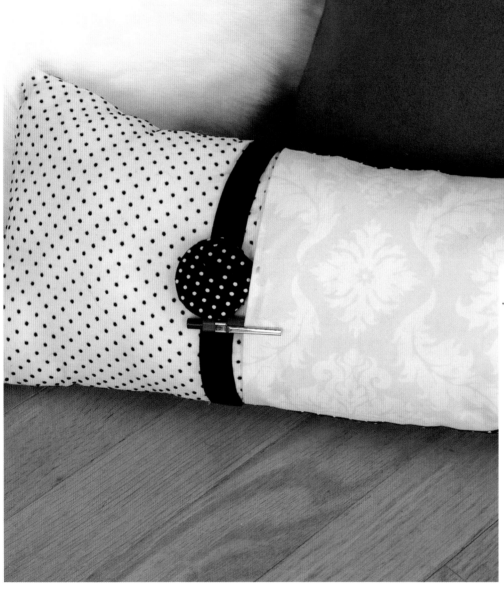

YOU'LL NEED:

- ¼ yard (45" wide) white fabric with black polka-dots
- ¼ yard (45" wide) damask cotton print
- ¼ yard (45" wide) black fabric with white polka-dots
- 9" piece (½" wide) black velvet ribbon
- 1 large self-coverable button
- 1 small bag Poly-fil
- 6" piece black elastic rope
- Sewing machine
- Iron and ironing board
- Stitch Kit (see page 14)

SKILL LEVEL **201**

Privacy Pocket Pillow

While she may turn out to be your best friend for life, a roommate in a small space often means no privacy. That's why this pillow, which can secretly stow a personal journal, a cash stash, or simply your jewelry, is perfect—and only you need to know about it.

Prepare the pieces.

1 From the white polka-dot fabric, cut:
1 front: 8" wide x 9" long

From the damask, cut:
1 front: 13" wide x 9" long
1 pocket: 26" wide x 9" long

From the black polka-dot fabric, cut:
1 back: 19" wide x 9" long

2 Pin the 9" ends of the front pieces together, **Wrong** sides together, and stitch a ¼" seam.

3 Fold the damask pocket piece in half along its width, so it measures 13" x 9".

Pin the pieces.

4 Place the pocket over the damask side of the front pillow piece, **Right**-sides up, so that the fold meets the seam line. Pin them together at the center of the pocket.

5 Pin the velvet ribbon just outside the fold.

6 Cover the button with a small piece of black polka-dot fabric, according to the package instructions. Stitch to the center of the velvet ribbon as shown in the photo.

7 Place and pin the back piece over the front piece, Wrong sides together.

Stitch the pillow.

8 Stitch the front and back pieces together using a ½" seam allowance and leaving a 3" opening. Trim the corners on the diagonal.

9 Turn the pillow Right-side out and press. Fill it with Poly-fil and **slipstitch** the opening closed.

10 Stitch the 6" piece of elastic rope to the inside of the pocket fold, at the center, and loop it around the button.

WHY WE LOVE FELT!

▸ It has this natural sticking quality, making it so easy to manage when sewing.

▸ It's the perfect fabric for no-sew projects because it doesn't fray.

▸ It comes in loads of vibrant and neutral hues.

▸ It's cheap! And we LOVE that!

YOU'LL NEED:

▸ ¾ yard (60" wide) blue felt

▸ ¼ yard (60" wide) white felt

▸ 1 black **felt square**

▸ 18" x 18" pillow form

▸ Fabric glue (optional)

▸ Sewing machine

▸ Stitch Kit (see page 14)

SKILL LEVEL **101**

Stone's Throw Pillow

Inspired by Jonathan Adler, the interior designer famous for his pottery, pillows, and playful decor, these felt "stones" are so simple and modern you can use them to accent any pillow with the right contrast of color. We chose teal, black, and white, but you can opt for any cool combos, like white with pink and orange, or green and brown.

Cut the fabric.

1 From the blue felt, cut:
2 sides: 19" x 19"

2 On the white felt, using fabric chalk, draw a large stone shape (no wider than 14"), cut:
1 large stone shape

3 On the black **felt square**, using fabric chalk, draw a smaller stone shape, cut:
1 small stone shape

Stitch the pillow.

4 Place and pin the stones on the pillow's face, as shown in the photo, and straight-stitch ¼" from the edge of the stones in a matching thread.

5 Place and pin the pillow squares, **Right** sides facing, and stitch a ½" seam, leaving a 12" opening on one side.

6 Trim the corners on the diagonal and turn the pillow Right-side out.

7 Stuff the pillow form into the pillow case and **slipstitch** the opening closed.

No-sew option! Buy a throw pillow in a solid color and use fabric glue to adhere felt stones to the front of it.

Cozy Cocoon Pillow

As we were working on the cocoon lampshades, the proverbial lightbulb went off: Hey! We can use these felt butterflies and petals on pillows, too! That's just the kind of thinking we encourage. Try them on curtains, on bags, even string them together in a variety of colors for a cool art piece.

Cut the fabric.

1 From the blue felt, cut:
2 squares: 19" x 19"

2 From the white felt, using the cocoon template, trace and cut:
3 small butterflies
12 petals

3 From the black felt, cut:
1 long stem: 12" long x ¼" wide

1 medium stem: 9" long x ¼" wide
1 short stem: 5" long x ¼" wide

Stitch the pillow.

4 Pin, then stitch the pieces to the pillow's face as shown in the photo. Allow the butterfly wings to flutter.

5 Pin the pillow back to the front, **Right** sides facing. Stitch a ½" seam, leaving a 12" opening.

6 Trim the corners on the diagonal and turn the cover Right-side out.

7 Stuff the pillow form into the pillow cover and **slipstitch** the opening closed.

No-sew option! Use fabric glue to adhere black and white felt pieces to the front of a purchased pillow.

YOU'LL NEED:

- Cocoon template (small butterfly and petals)
- ¾ yard (60" wide) blue felt
- 1 white **felt square**
- 1 black felt square
- 18" x 18" pillow form
- Fabric glue (optional)
- Sewing machine
- Stitch Kit (see page 14)

SKILL LEVEL   101

No-Pet Policy Pillow

Miss Muffy? Pine for your pooch? Snuggle up to them for the long haul of semesters with pillows honoring their mugs. Find your favorite pic (c'mon, we know you're like a granny with her brag book) and print it on fabric. Go for classic black-and-white, or print it in color to give those goofy dog sweaters their due.

Print the photo.

1 Using photo-editing software, extract the image from its background and enlarge it so it measures roughly 8" x 18".

2 Because the inkjet sheets are smaller than the pillow, you're going to have to print your photo on two inkjet sheets and then match them up. First, crop the top quarter of the image off and save the shorter photo as a new file. Undo that crop, then crop the bottom quarter from the full image and save this shorter one as another new file.

3 Following the manufacturer's instructions, print the cropped images onto two inkjet sheets (choosing portrait or landscape settings to allow a 2" border around the photo).

Stitch the pillow.

4 Match up the two inkjet sheets at the center so that you have one image (you'll need to fold the top sheet under so the pictures can overlap). Iron over the front of the image to make a crease—this will be your seam marker. (You'll also set the ink).

5 Pin the inkjet sheets together, **Wrong** sides facing (except for where the top image is folded under), and stitch along the fold line where the images line up. Trim the **seam allowance** to ¼".

6 **Right** sides together, place the inkjet sheet on the fabric and pin.

7 Use fabric chalk to mark the area around the image that you want to stitch, leaving 2" from the image's edge where possible. Leave a 6" opening at the bottom.

8 Stitch along the marked line, then trim the **seam allowance** to ¼".

9 Press the seams flat, clipping at the curves, and turn the pillow Right-side out.

10 Fill the pillow with Poly-fil, then stitch the opening closed.

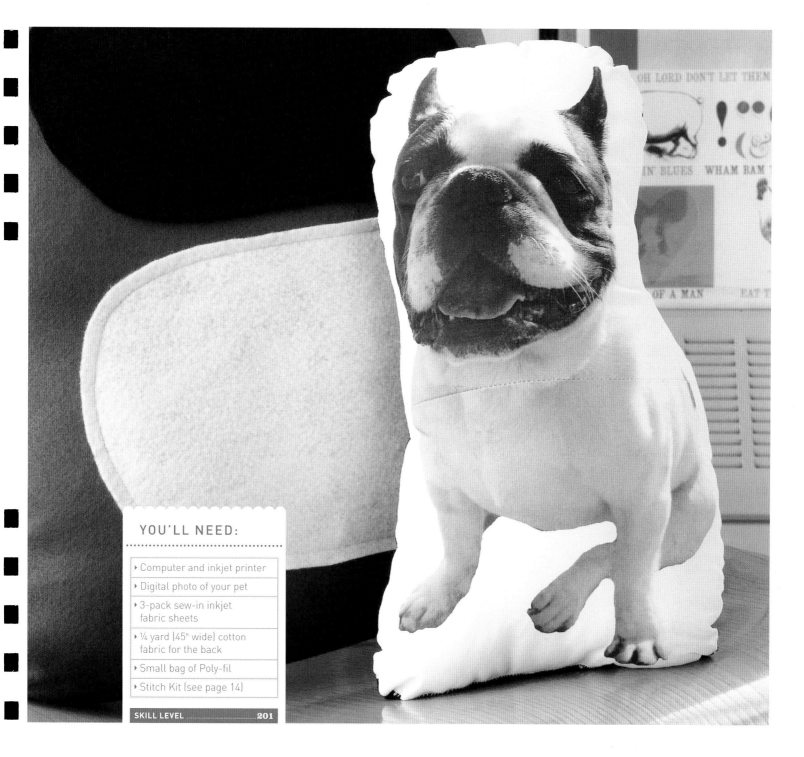

WHERE YOU DRESS

Rummaging through closet clutter when you're late for class can be a real drag. Keep those never-find-'em-when-you-need-'em items always within reach with projects that help you put your pretty little things in the right places.

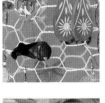

Hanging Closet Organizer

Fashion meets home decor with one practical frock. A mod-inspired silhouette of fray-free felt makes this closet organizer super-easy—and baubles along the neckline show you can organize in style.

Cut the dress.

1 Fold the felt in half along its width so that you have at least 29" of fabric from the fold.

2 Place and pin the dress template on the felt, meeting the shoulders to the felt's fold line. Cut along the template cut lines, leaving the shoulders uncut at the top.

3 Fold the **interfacing** in half and pin the dress template to it. Cut along the interfacing cut line. Iron the interfacing on the **Wrong** side of the felt around the neck and shoulders.

Make the pockets.

4 From the pink cotton, cut:
1 large pocket piece: 18" wide x 15" long

5 Fold the fabric lengthwise sides in half, **Right** sides together. Press. Trace the large pocket template onto the fabric, matching the fold line to the fold.

6 Trace the pattern onto the interfacing and cut it out. Iron interfacing to the Wrong side of the fabric piece (the untraced side).

7 Pin the Right sides together, then trim ½" from the trace line. Stitch along the trace line, leaving a 3" opening. Turn it Right-side out and press.

8 Fold the opening inside and pin.

9 Pin the pocket to the dress's front, as shown in the photo.

10 Repeat steps 3 to 8 for all the other patterns, using a 15"-wide x 13"-long piece of pink cotton for the medium pocket and a 6"-wide x 12"-long piece of pink cotton for each small pocket.

11 **Topstitch** the pockets to the felt along the bottom and sides only.

Cover the buttons.

12 According to the package's instructions, cover the buttons with polka-dot and houndstooth fabrics: 3 small black/white and white/black each;

continued

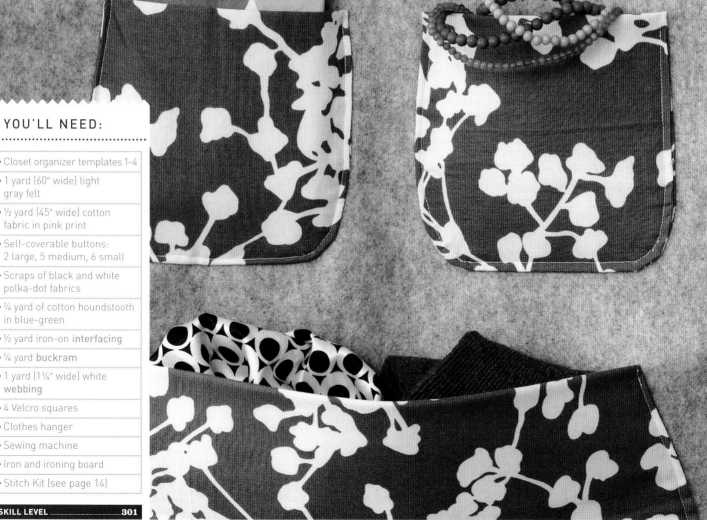

YOU'LL NEED:

- ▸ Closet organizer templates 1–4
- ▸ 1 yard (60" wide) light gray felt
- ▸ ½ yard (45" wide) cotton fabric in pink print
- ▸ Self-coverable buttons: 2 large, 5 medium, 6 small
- ▸ Scraps of black and white polka-dot fabrics
- ▸ ¼ yard of cotton houndstooth in blue-green
- ▸ ½ yard iron-on **interfacing**
- ▸ ¼ yard **buckram**
- ▸ 1 yard (1¼" wide) white **webbing**
- ▸ 4 Velcro squares
- ▸ Clothes hanger
- ▸ Sewing machine
- ▸ Iron and ironing board
- ▸ Stitch Kit (see page 14)

SKILL LEVEL 301

2 medium houndstooth and 1 white/
black; 1 large black/white and houndstooth each. Stitch to the pockets and
neckline as shown in the photo or as
desired.

13 According to the package instructions,
cover 2 medium buttons with black/
white polka-dot fabric. Set aside.

Stitch the belt holder.

14 From the **buckram**, cut:
2 pieces: 16" wide x 1" long

Stitch 1 piece to the back of a 16"-long
piece of **webbing**. Set the other piece
aside.

15 From the houndstooth, cut:
1 piece: 19" wide x 3" long

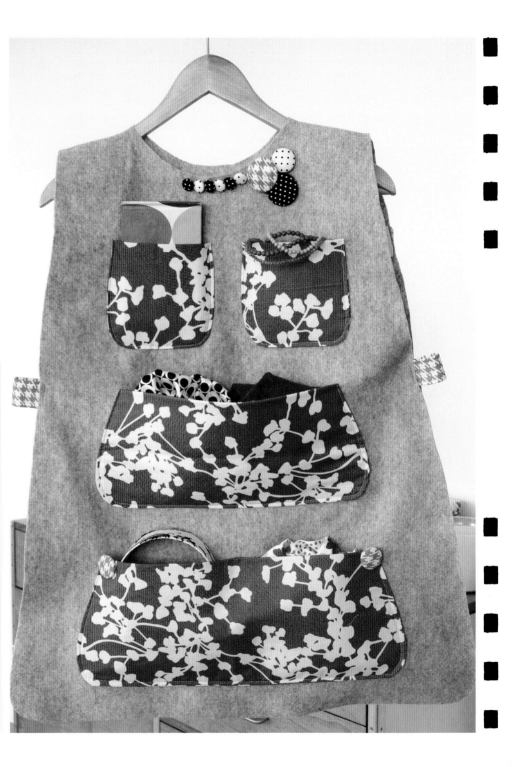

Center the webbing (buckram-side up) over the Wrong side of the houndstooth and pin the fabric over the webbing to cover (pressing the raw edges under). Stitch along both long sides, leaving at least 1" of fabric on both short ends.

16 Fold the short ends over to the Wrong side of the belt, fold the raw edges under, and stitch.

17 Pin the webbing to the back of the dress as shown in the photo (making sure the ends meet the edge of the dress). Pin the second strip of buckram on the Wrong side of the dress, matching it up behind the belt placement. This will ensure a strong hold.

18 Remove the belt and set it aside. Stitch the buckram to the dress along the center width (the long side).

19 Pin the belt back in place and stitch at the center lengthwise (to cross the back stitching), leaving two ends unstitched.

20 Hand-sew one black and one white polka-dot button over each end of the belt (not to the dress).

21 Place a Velcro square on the Wrong side of each end, and one between each end and the center stitch line.

Sew the side loops.

22 From the 1¼"-wide webbing, cut: 2 pieces: 4" long

From the houndstooth, cut: 2 pieces: 5" wide x 3" long

Cover the webbing as described in steps 15 and 16.

23 Fold the pieces in half, Wrong sides together, to create a loop, and pin ½" into the sides of the dress (as shown in the photo), through both dress sides. This will keep the dress in place on the hanger.

24 Using thread the color of the dress, stitch a square around the end of the tabs, through both layers of the dress.

25 Place the hanger through the neck of the dress and hang!

60 WHERE YOU DRESS

Dorm Decor **60**

YOU'LL NEED:

YOU'LL NEED:

‣ Gardening gloves

‣ 22" x 12" poultry wire (for a 7"-diameter column); 32" x 12" (for a 9"-diameter column)

‣ Wire cutters (go low-end; poultry wire is pretty thin)

‣ 1 can of white spray paint

‣ Newspaper or plastic bags

‣ 1 yard ½"-wide **grosgrain ribbon** in raspberry

‣ Two Velcro squares

‣ 10 craft birds with wire hooks

SKILL LEVEL **101**

Jewelry Chandelier

For a place to put all that glitters, think outside the jewelry box (charming tunes, yes, but they can create a tangled mess) and visit your local hardware store. The honeycomb shape of this poultry wire alludes to something fanciful, yet utterly practical. To dress it up, a can of spray paint, ribbon, and colorful craft birds do the trick.

Cut the wire.

1 You may need to purchase the poultry wire in a package (not custom cut to size). Wearing gloves, make sure to cut along the seam line so stray wires are not exposed.

2 Join the 22" ends of the poultry wire together to form a cylinder. Interlace the wire ends through the loops on the other end to secure it closed.

Paint the wire.

3 In a ventilated area (preferably outside) and over newspaper or plastic, spray the cylinder with white paint according to the manufacturer's instructions. Apply two coats for even coverage.

Embellish the chandelier.

4 Cut the ribbon in half and cut each Velcro square in half.

5 Loop one ribbon through the wire at one point at the top. Use half a Velcro square on the end of the ribbon to close the loop. Determine the length you want the chandelier to hang and snip any extra ribbon. Directly across the top, loop the other end of the ribbon and use the other half of the Velcro square to close up the ribbon (this way you can hang it on a closet pole or remove the ribbon to set the chandelier on a dresser). Repeat for the other ribbon and Velcro square across the top.

6 Attach the craft birds with hooks on the chandelier as desired.

7 Hang the chandelier from a window hook, above your dresser, or in your closet. Hang your jewelry on it, any way you like.

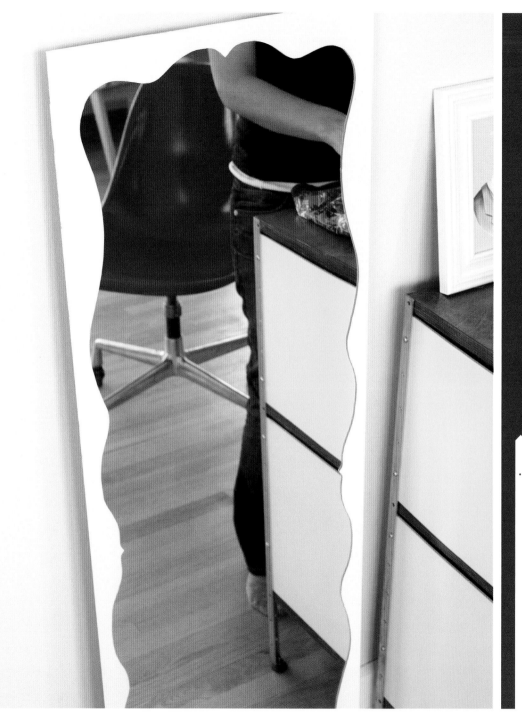

P.S. One of the most famous baroque palaces, the Palace of Versailles in France, features a Hall of Mirrors (or *Galerie des Glaces*) with 357 spectacular mirrors!

YOU'LL NEED:

- Mirror template
- Full-length mirror (ideally frameless; template fits a 15 ¾" x 47" mirror but can be enlarged or reduced to fit any mirror)
- Double-sided tape
- White paint marker
- 8 oz. can of white enamel paint
- Fine paintbrush
- Small sponge paintbrush

SKILL LEVEL **101**

Baroque (for the Broke) Mirror

Baroque, and later Rococo, styles of the 17th and 18th centuries were rooted in ornamentation and curves—think Marie Antoinette and all her excess. But gilded gaudiness seems a little overdone for a small dorm room. Evoke the look by adding a crisp white border to a full-length frameless mirror for what we like to call "Opulence on a Budget."

Prepare the pattern.

1 First make sure your mirror is clean and dry. Then measure the template to your mirror, making sure it fits evenly on all four corners. You may need to enlarge or minimize it on a photo copier to fit your mirror.

2 Tape the template onto a corner of your mirror as seen in the photo or as desired.

Paint the pattern.

3 With the mirror on the floor, trace the template onto the four corners of the mirror with a paint marker.

4 Once the paint is dry, remove the template. Paint inside the pattern with enamel paint, using the fine paintbrush for curves and the sponge brush for the larger areas. Retouch the pattern with a paint marker when the paint is dry.

YOU'LL NEED:

- ⅓ yard (45" wide) cotton print fabric
- ¼ yard (45" wide) contrasting cotton print fabric
- ½ yard (½" wide) sew-in Velcro
- 1½ yards (⅜" wide) twill tape for tie
- 1¼ yards (⅜" wide) elastic in white
- ⅔ yard (½" wide) double-fold **bias tape**
- Sewing machine
- Iron and ironing board
- Stitch Kit (see page 14)

SKILL LEVEL **301**

Cosmetics Carryall

Product junkies, unite! This nooks-and-crannies tote is designed to hold everything, from your moisturizers and blushes to your eyeliners and shadows. Now you can hide your addiction to lipgloss—it'll all be tucked neatly away.

P.S. If the stress of classes starts to take a toll on your skin, try this dorm-made recipe: Simply run a honey packet under warm water to heat it, then apply the warm honey to your face. After a couple of minutes, rinse with warm water, then cool water. Works great for all skin types!

Cut the fabric.
(Use a ½" **seam allowance**)

1 From the main print fabric, cut:
2 small pieces: 6" x 11"
1 large piece: 17" x 11"

From the contrasting fabric, cut:
1 piece: 7" x 11"

Sew the outside of the pouch.

2 Pin one small piece of the main print fabric to the piece of contrasting fabric, **Right** sides facing, lining up one 11" edge. Machine-sew the 11" edge, then press the seam open. Repeat to sew the second small piece to the other end of the contrasting fabric. This is your outside piece.

3 Fold the unstitched 11" edges of the outside piece to the **Wrong** side by ½" and press (See illustration, page 67).

4 Cut the Velcro in half to create two 9" pieces. Separate the hook side and the loop side.

5 Place the hook side over the raw edge on one end of the outside piece on the Wrong side of the fabric and pin it in place. Repeat on the other raw edge.

continued

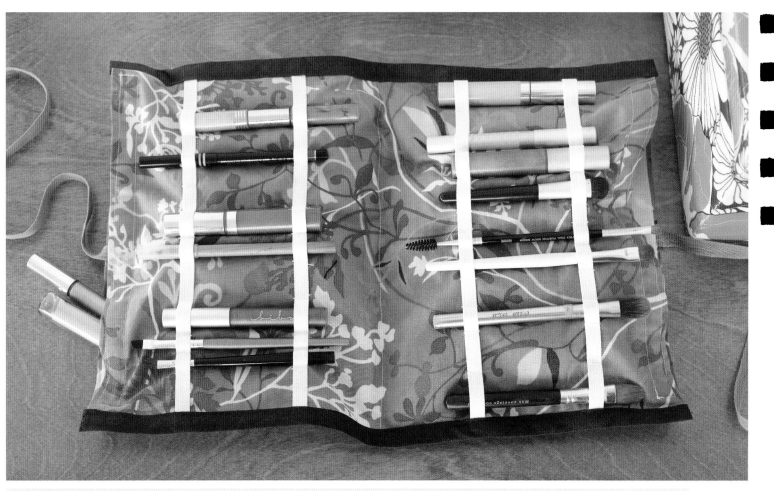

6 Cut the twill tape into one 1-yard piece and one ½-yard piece. Pin one piece of the twill tape underneath the Velcro on one end of the outside pouch piece as shown in the illustration, and pin the second piece of twill tape under the Velcro on the other end of the pouch.

7 Sew the Velcro pieces down around the edges of the Velcro.

Sew the inside pieces.

8 Fold both 11" edges of the 17" x 11" piece to the Wrong side by ½" and press. Place the two loop pieces of the Velcro over the raw 11" edges (just like you did in step 5) and machine-sew it in place around the edges of the Velcro.

9 Cut the elastic into 4 pieces, each 11" long. Arrange the pieces on the Right side of the pouch inside piece of fabric, as shown in the illustration. Space the center two elastic pieces approximately 4½" apart and 3" away from the outermost pieces.

10 Mark on the elastic pieces where you would like them to be secured down.

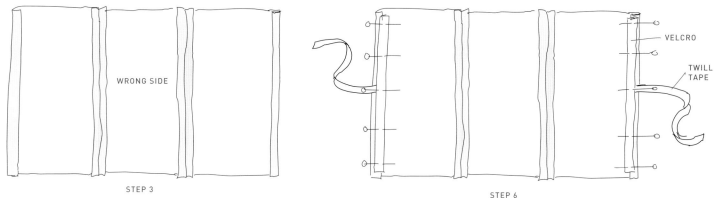

WRONG SIDE

STEP 3

VELCRO

TWILL TAPE

STEP 6

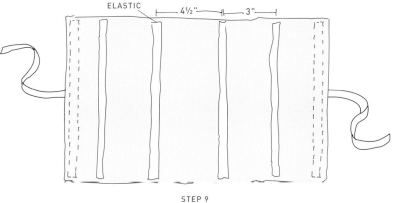

ELASTIC

4½" 3"

STEP 9

For example, mark approximately ½" for eyeliner pencils, and 1" for mascara and larger tubes. Just make sure that the two pieces to the left side of the center are identical and the two pieces to the right of the center are identical. Machine-sew the elastic in place along the markings.

Finish the bag.

11 Pin the inside to the outside piece, matching the raw edges, with the Wrong sides facing. Stitch the 16" edges together with a ½" seam allowance.

12 Fold the bag in half, matching the 11" edges, and mark the center fold with

pins. Unfold the bag and stitch down the marked center through both layers.

13 Cut the **bias tape** into two 17" pieces. Press the raw edges of the bias tape to the Wrong side by ½". Pin each piece along each 16" edge of the bag and machine-sew it in place, close to the inside edge of the tape.

Oh Dear, Deer Head

For the animal lover, activist, or simply anyone with a sense of humor, this faux buck will make any dorm-room dweller proud. Hang a scarf or hat on his antlers, keeping floors free and clear, or use him as witty wall art. For more tips on cutting foam core, turn to page 16.

Make the pieces.

1 Using the deer templates:
From the ³⁄₁₆" thick foam core, cut:
1 deer antlers
2 deer heads
1 deer body
1 deer nose

From the ½" thick foam core, cut:
1 mounting board

Cover the pieces.

2 Using spray adhesive, spray one side of the nose piece and adhere it to the **Wrong**-side of the wrapping paper. Use the craft knife and the cutting board and cut out the nose piece. Repeat for the other side of the nose.

3 Repeat to cover both sides of the two deer heads, the deer body, and the deer antler pieces.

4 Using spray adhesive, adhere the contrasting paper to one side of the mounting board. Cut it out using the craft knife and cutting board.

Hang the deer head.

5 On each deer head piece, cut a hole 1" below the top edge and ³⁄₈" inside the back edge with the awl.

6 Assemble the deer head as shown in the photograph.

7 Thread wire through both holes several times and end by wrapping the wire around itself for a hanger.

YOU'LL NEED:

....

- Deer templates 1–5
- One 20" x 30" piece ($3/_{16}$" thick) foam core
- One 6" x 7" piece (½" thick) foam core
- 60" length (30" wide) wrapping paper
- One 6" x 7" piece of contrasting paper
- Spray adhesive
- Craft knife
- Cutting board
- Awl
- Picture-frame hanging wire

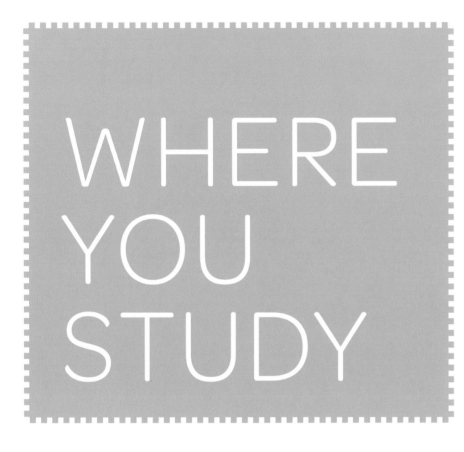

WHERE YOU STUDY

Let your genius, not your mess, shine through with projects that keep your desk clear (and comfy). Craft three-in-one fabric boxes for all your desktop supplies, a sweet cushion for late-night cramming (so you stay on the dean's list and off the D list!), and a roomy messenger bag to haul heavy textbooks around campus.

YOU'LL NEED:

‣ Corkboard template
‣ 4 tiles of 24" x 12" corkboard
‣ Tracing pencil
‣ Craft knife
‣ Cutting mat
‣ Sticky Tack hanging adhesive

SKILL LEVEL **101**

Silhouette Message Board

Post your favorite postcards, photos, and phone numbers (hee hee) or keep all your syllabi in clear view with this absolutely fab corkboard. It's so easy, you can cut out more than one (for personal and for serious school stuff) or turn it into a faux headboard simply by changing the size of the template. For tips on using a craft knife, turn to page 16.

Cut out the board.

1 From the corkboard tiles, using the silhouette template, trace and cut: 4 pieces (Be sure to cut on the cutting mat.)

Assemble the board.

2 Arrange the board pieces on your wall as pictured. Hang on the wall using Sticky Tack adhesive or removable mounting strips.

Tufted Seat Cushion

The last thing you want when you're trying to get in study mode is an uncomfortable chair. Give your tush more cush with a tufted seat so you can study (or chat online) all night long.

Cut the pieces.

(Use a ½" **seam allowance**.)

1. From the fabric, cut:
   2 pieces: 13" x 13"
   4 sides: 13" x 3½"

Add the piping.

2. Using fabric chalk and a ruler, mark a line ½" in from all of the edges on the **Right** side of both 13" x 13" fabric pieces. Pin the **piping** onto one of the 13" x 13" pieces. Make sure the seam of the piping is on top of your chalk line as shown in the illustration. When you get to a corner, clip the lip of the piping to make a nice turn. Overlap the ends of the piping by 1", turning the raw ends toward the raw edge of the fabric piece.

3. Load your sewing machine with a **zipper foot**. Sew the piping onto the fabric, using the zipper foot as a guide to stitch close to the piping all the way around.

4. Add piping to the second 13" x 13" piece the same way.

Connect the sides.

5. Load the machine with a regular **presser foot**. Pin two 13" x 3½" pieces together with the Right sides facing and the raw edges even. Sew one 3½" side together, starting and stopping your stitching ½" away from the top and bottom edges. Press the seam open. Repeat to attach all four 13" x 3½" pieces together to form a large circle.

6. Pin the side pieces to one 13" x 13" piece with the Right sides facing and the raw edges even. At each corner, fan out the seam allowance as pictured in the illustration. Load your machine with a zipper foot and sew the sides to the larger piece, stitching close to the piping.

7. Repeat to connect the second 13" x 13" piece, but leave an 8" opening on one side.

Finish the cushion.

8. Clip the corners of the pillowcase close to the stitching. Turn the case Right-side out and press. Insert the foam cushion.

9. Slipstitch the opening closed using a hand-sewing needle and thread.

Tuft the cushion.

10. Following the manufacturer's instructions, cover the buttons with white fabric. Using fabric chalk, mark on the pillow where you would like your buttons.

11. Thread the upholstery needle with two strands of waxed button-thread and push it through the marking on your pillow, leaving a 4" to 6" tail, coming out on the other side of the pillow. Pass the needle through the shank of one button, then, going through the same hole in the form, pass the needle back through the pillow and through the shank of the second button. Remove the needle and tie the thread ends together, pulling the thread taught. Tie again around the button shank and cut off the excess. Repeat with the other buttons.

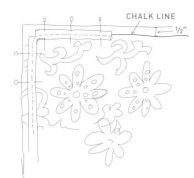

CHALK LINE ⟶ ½"

STEP 2

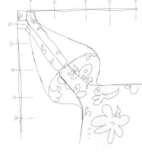

STEP 6

YOU'LL NEED:

▸ ⅜ yard (45" wide) cotton fabric
▸ 2¾ yards **piping** in a contrasting color
▸ 8 (1⅛" diameter) coverable buttons and white fabric to cover, or 8 white buttons
▸ 12" x 12" x 2½" foam cushion
▸ Upholstery needle
▸ Waxed button-thread
▸ Sewing machine
▸ Iron and ironing board
▸ Stitch Kit (page 14)

SKILL LEVEL   201

EXTRA CREDIT! Enlarge the dimensions of this project to make a large floor cushion, great for movie night or study groups.

P.S. We went city style with brownstone-inspired buildings, but you could paint whatever you like on the rectangular shape. Robots, logos, sports fields, maps, or just abstract patterns would be cool.

YOU'LL NEED:

- ¼ yard (45" wide) cotton fabric for the house
- ¼ yard (45" wide) cotton fabric for the roof
- Fabric paints in white, orange, brown, and black
- Paintbrush
- Newspaper
- 2 lbs. of Poly-Pellets, rice, or sand for stuffing
- Sewing machine
- Iron and ironing board
- Stitch Kit (see page 14)

SKILL LEVEL   201

Building Bookends

Keep books off the floor and within reach with these clever bookends. Simply fill the case with Poly-Pellets, dry rice, beans, or sand. They make great doorstops, too—or you can enlarge the instructions for a cinderblock cozy. Simply revise the dimensions in step 1 based on the size of your block, leave the bottom unstitched, and place the cozy over the cinderblock before propping it under your bed.

Cut and paint the pieces.
(Use a ½" **seam allowance**.)

1 From the house fabric, cut:
4 sides: 8" x 7"

From the roof fabric, cut:
1 top: 7" x 7"
1 bottom: 7" x 7"
4 roof sides: 4" x 7"

2 Lay one house piece and the four roof side pieces on the newspaper. To paint a door and window motif onto the house piece, first paint the white in the window, orange in the door, and brown in the steps. Let that dry before painting a second layer, if needed. then paint the black outlines. Let dry.

3 On the roof pieces, paint the shingles in black as pictured in the photo. It's okay if these lines aren't perfect. Let dry.

Assemble the building

4 Pin each house side to a roof side, matching 7" edges (make sure that the roof is pinned to the top edge of the house's side). Sew each seam on the sewing machine. Press the seams open.

5 Pin each building side to another, matching the raw edges, with the **Right** sides facing. Sew each seam, starting and stopping ½" from the top and bottom.

6 Pin the top onto the building with the Right sides facing and the raw edges even. Fan out the seam allowance of the sides at each corner to get around the top piece evenly. Machine-sew all four sides. Trim the corners.

7 Pin the bottom onto the building and sew it in the same manner, leaving a 4" opening on one edge.

Stuff the building.

8 Turn the building Right-side out. Fill the building with Poly-Pellets, sand, rice, or other weighted filler.

9 **Slipstitch** the opening shut.

Quilted Laptop-Cozy

Protect your most valuable college possession with this snug-as-a-bug quilted cover. With its straight quilting lines, it's the perfect project for first-time quilters. Use it when you're on the go (it fits well in our Messenger Book Bag on page 84) or for storing your laptop at home (guarding the computer from any accidental spills). You can even turn this cozy into a tote; simply flip to the Messenger Book Bag instructions for details on adding a strap.

Cozy will fit one 13" x 10" x 1¼" laptop. Adjust where necessary to fit your laptop.

Cut the pieces.

1 Using the cozy template:
From the teal fabric, cut:
1 cozy piece

From the green fabric, cut:
1 cozy piece

From the **batting**, cut:
1 cozy piece

Transfer all markings onto the green fabric using fabric chalk.

Quilt the pieces.

2 Sandwich the batting between the green and teal fabrics. Adhere the layers together using temporary spray adhesive or safety pins. If you use safety pins, be sure to pin between the stitch lines, so that you won't accidentally stitch over them.

3 Load the sewing machine with a **walking foot**. Set the stitch on the machine to about 3.5 mm.

4 Sew through all the layers along the stitch lines, quilting the layers together.

Assemble the cozy.

5 Load the machine with a regular **presser foot**. Stitch around the edges of the cozy piece with a ½" **seam allowance** through all the layers.

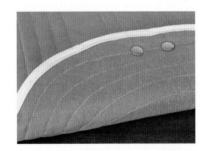

6 Cut a 15" piece of **bias tape**. Pin it to the short, straight end of the cozy piece, sandwiching the raw edges inside the bias tape. Stitch the tape in place along the inside folded edge, making sure you stitch through the back side of the bias tape at the same time.

7 Fold the cozy along the fold line with the teal sides facing each other, and pin in place. Pin the remaining bias

YOU'LL NEED:

- Laptop cozy template
- ½ yard (45" wide) cotton fabric in teal
- ½ yard (45" wide) cotton fabric in green
- 26" x 15" high-loft **batting**
- 1²/₃ yards (³/₈" wide) double-fold **bias tape** in yellow
- 2 (⁵/₈" diameter) heavy-duty snaps
- Temporary spray adhesive or safety pins
- Sewing machine
- Walking **presser foot** for sewing machine (optional, but very helpful)
- Iron and ironing board
- Stitch Kit (see page 14)

tape around the raw edge of the cozy, sandwiching the raw edges inside the bias tape. Stitch the tape in place along the inside folded edge, making sure you stitch through the back side of the bias tape at the same time. At each end of the bias tape, turn under ½" to hide the raw edge.

8 Slip the laptop into the cozy and close the flap. Mark with fabric chalk where you would like the snaps. Following the manufacturer's instructions, attach the snaps to the cozy.

Desktop Catchall

You can never have too much storage. Thankfully, these 3-in-1 boxes take care of the small stuff—pencils, computer paper, staples—all in one pretty package. A handy pocket inside makes losing eyeglasses, business cards (hey, you never know), or keys history, too.

Makes two 8" x 5" boxes and one 9" x 12" box.

Cut the foam core.

1. Use a pencil to label the size of each piece before cutting. On the foam core, mark:
   1 piece: 9" x 11½"
   2 pieces: 2½" x 11½"
   2 pieces: 9" x 2½"
   5 pieces: 5" x 5"
   6 pieces: 5" x 8"

2. Using a ruler and craft knife, cut the pieces out of foam core. (Follow the tips on page 16.)

Prepare the large paper box.

3. From the green cotton, cut:
   2 pieces: 17" x 19½"

   Place the pieces **Right** sides together.

4. Place one 9" x 11½", two 9" x 2½", and two 2½" x 11½" foam pieces over the **Wrong** side of the fabric pieces as shown in the illustration on page 83. Leave ¼" between the facing 9" sides.

5. At the corners, use fabric chalk to mark a square along the foam core pieces, ⅛" from the edges.

Stitch the large paper box.

6. Pin at the mark lines and remove the foam core pieces.

7. Stitch ⅛" from the marked lines toward the outside edge. Trim ¼" from the stitch lines and put the fabric squares aside.

8. Press the seam lines flat and turn the fabric cover Right-side out.

continued

YOU'LL NEED:

- 24" x 36" (¼" thick) foam core
- 1 yard (45" wide) cotton print in green and white
- ½ yard (45" wide) cotton print in light blue polka-dot
- 2 yards (½" wide) velvet ribbon in teal
- 2 medium self-coverable buttons
- Scrap of polka-dot fabric in brown
- 1 package double-fold **bias tape** in brown
- Fabric glue
- Pencil
- Straight-edge ruler (preferably metal)
- Craft knife and blade
- Craft cutting board
- Sewing machine with a **cording foot**
- Iron and ironing board
- Stitch Kit (see page 14)

SKILL LEVEL 301

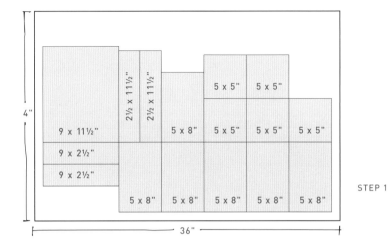
STEP 1

9 Place the 9" x 11½" foam inside the center. Using chalk, mark around the foam piece on the side that will be the box's inside. Remove the foam.

10 Stitch around the two long ends and one short end mark at the center.

11 Replace the foam piece at the center and, using a **cording foot**, stitch the center closed.

Finish the large box.

12 Place the remaining four foam core pieces at the sides. Pinning the box in place, take one side, tuck in the fabric at the top, and glue the fabric closed (fabric glue is strong; you don't need a lot, so make sure glue does not flow out to the fabric). Repeat for all sides.

13 Hand-stitch two corners together until the pieces form a box.

14 Using fabric glue, glue the **bias tape** over the top edges all around the box, folding the ends under.

Prepare the small paper box.

15 From the green cotton, cut:
1 piece: 20½" x 18"

From the blue cotton, cut:
1 piece: 20½" x 18"

Place the pieces Right sides together.

16 Place one 5" x 8" foam piece at the center of the fabric's Wrong side. Place one 5" x 8" piece to the right and one to the left of that center piece, matching the 8" sides. Place one 5" x 5" piece at the top andon at the bottom, matching the 5" sides. Leave ¼" between the facing sides.

17 At the corners, use fabric chalk to mark a square along the foam core pieces, ⅛" from the edges.

Stitch the small paper box.

18 Insert pins at the mark lines and remove the foam core pieces.

19 Stitch ⅛" from the mark lines toward the outside edge. Trim the **seam allowance** to ¼" and put the fabric squares aside.

20 Press the seam lines flat and turn the fabric cover inside out.

21 Place one 5" x 8" foam piece inside the center of the fabric cover. Using chalk, mark around the foam piece on the side that will be the inside of the box. Remove the foam.

22 Stitch around the two long ends and one short end mark at the center.

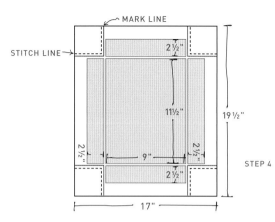

MARK LINE

STITCH LINE →

2½"

11½"

19½"

2½"

9"

2½"

2½"

STEP 4

17"

23 Replace the foam piece at the center and, using a cording foot, stitch the center closed.

Finish the small box.

24 Place the remaining four foam core pieces at the sides. Pinning the box in place, take one side, tuck in the fabric at the top, and glue the fabric closed. Repeat for all sides.

25 At each corner, hand-stitch two sides together at the top point until the pieces form a box.

26 Wrap velvet ribbon around the box, overlapping by 2" at front. Glue the ribbon to the box, and trim the ribbon's end in a V-shape.

27 Cover one button with polka-dot fabric, according to the manufacturer's

instructions. Glue the button to the box's front as seen in the photograph on page 81.

Make the pencil box.

28 Repeat steps 15 to 27 for the small box.

29 From the green fabric, cut:
1 piece: 6" x 12"

Fold it lengthwise, Right sides facing (so you have a 6" x 6" square).

30 Center the remaining 5" x 5" piece of foam over the Wrong side of the fabric piece, with the top edge against the fabric's fold.

31 Using fabric chalk, use the foam as a template to mark the left and right sides. Stitch ⅛" outside the mark lines. Press the seams flat and turn the fabric pocket inside out.

32 Place the 5" x 5" foam core inside the fabric pocket. Turn the bottom ends in and glue them closed.

33 Glue all three sides of the piece (leaving the seamless side unglued and at top) and carefully place inside the small box (avoid spreading the glue).

34 For the pocket, take a 6" x 6" scrap from a green and a blue corner. Place the Right sides together and stitch ¼" from the edge along three sides. Press the seams flat and turn the pocket Right-side out. Press again and stitch ¼" all around. Glue three ends on the Wrong side and press against the inner side of the box.

Messenger Book Bag

Running from class to class with everything but the kitchen sink can be a long haul. This messenger-style book bag makes it easier by hanging comfortably across your body and putting your cell phone, pencils, and other necessities within reach in a handy pocket. But the best part? You can make it out of any fabric that suits your style.

Cut the pieces.

1 From the outside fabric, cut:
1 piece: 16 ½" x 17"

From the lining fabric, cut:
1 piece: 16 ½" x 17"

From the **interfacing**, cut:
2 pieces: 16 ½" x 17"

Following the manufacturer's instructions, fuse the interfacing onto the **Wrong** side of each fabric piece. Layer the pieces on top of each other and pin together. Trim two corners along one 17" edge to create a slight curve at each corner. Unpin the pieces. These will form the flap.

2 From the outside fabric, cut:
1 piece: 13" x 17"

From the lining fabric, cut:
1 piece: 13" x 17"

From the interfacing, cut:
2 pieces: 13" x 17"

Fuse the interfacing onto the Wrong side of each fabric piece. These will be the back pieces.

3 From the outside fabric, cut:
1 piece: 12 ½" x 17"

From the lining fabric, cut:
1 piece: 12 ½" x 17"

From the interfacing, cut:
1 pieces: 12 ½" x 17"

Fuse the interfacing onto the Wrong side of each piece. These will be the inside pieces.

4 From the outside fabric, cut:
1 piece: 40" x 6"

From the lining fabric, cut:
1 piece: 40" x 6"

From the interfacing, cut:
2 pieces: 40" x 6"

Fuse the interfacing onto the Wrong side of each piece. These will be the side pieces.

5 From the lining fabric, cut:
1 pocket: 12" x 7 ½"

Stitch the pocket.

6 Fold the pocket in half, matching the 7 ½" edges. With the **Right** sides facing. Sew the raw edges together using a ¼" **seam allowance**, leaving 3" unstitched.

continued

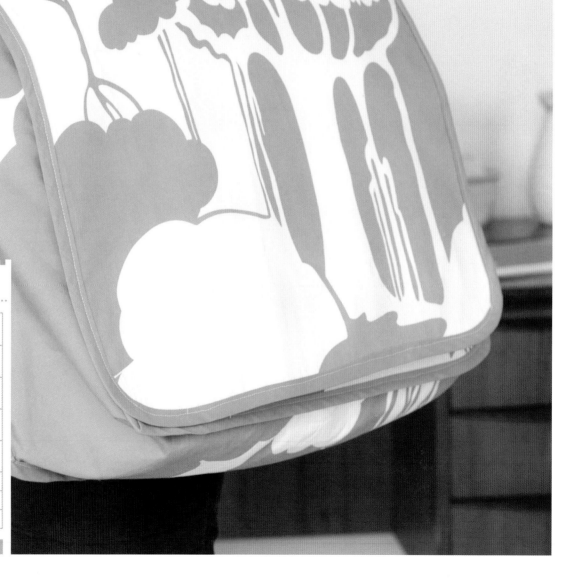

SKILL LEVEL **301**

Dorm Decor

| ← ¾" → |

STEP 7

Trim the corners and turn the pocket Right-side out. Press the pocket and **slipstitch** the opening closed.

7 Center the pocket on the piece of the outside fabric you cut in step 3. **Topstitch** the pocket in place around its sides and bottom edge. To create pencil pouches in the pocket, top-stitch three more parallel lines, ¾" apart, parallel to the sides of the pocket (as shown in the illustration).

Assemble the pieces.

8 Pin the flap piece of the outside fabric to the back piece of the outside fabric, matching 17" edges, with Right sides facing. Machine-sew with a ½" seam allowance. Press the seam open. Repeat for the lining pieces.

9 Pin each of the outside fabric pieces to its matching lining piece with Wrong sides facing. **Baste** the pieces together with the sewing machine around the edges of each piece using a ¼" seam allowance.

10 Cut a 17" piece of **bias tape** and pin it along the top edge of the inside bag piece, sandwiching the edge inside the bias tape. Machine-sew in place along the bias tape's inside edge, making sure to stitch through the back of the bias tape as well.

11 Cut two 6" pieces of bias tape and pin them along each 6" edge of the side piece, sandwiching the raw edges inside the bias tape. Machine-sew in place along the inside edge of the bias tape,

making sure that you are also stitching through the back of the bias tape.

12 Pin the side piece to the inside piece, Wrong sides facing. Each end of the side piece should be even with the top edge of the inside piece. Sew together using a ½" seam allowance.

13 Pin the other side of the side piece to the back piece. Each end of the side piece should be even with the seam that connects the back piece to the flap. Sew together using a ½" seam allowance.

14 Use the remaining bias tape to pin around the rest of the raw edges of the bag and stitch in place. At each end of the bias tape, turn the end under ½" to hide the raw edge.

Attach the strap.

15 Fold each end of the **webbing** under 2" and press in place. With the raw edge of each end of the strap face-down, pin each end of the strap 3" below the top edge of each end side piece. (Make sure the strap isn't twisted before pinning.)

16 Stitch the strap to the bag in the shape of a 1½" x 2" rectangle. Stitch across the center of the rectangle from corner to corner to create a stitched "X" within the rectangle.

Magritte Pencil Pouch

Inspired by the amusing artwork of René Magritte, this pouch tucks small things away with a smirk. Use it for more than just pencils (money, makeup, art supplies, notions, laundry change). For an embroidery primer, turn to page 19.

Embroider the design.

(Use a ¼" **seam allowance**.)

1. Transfer the pouch template onto the green fabric using the carbon paper and **tracing wheel**, making sure you leave at least 1½" of room around the edges of the design.

2. Mount the design into your embroidery hoop.

3. Thread the embroidery needle with three strands of embroidery floss.

4. Embroider the design using your desired stitches. We used the backstitch for the letters, outline, and lines in the pencil; satin stitch on the eraser and the tip of the pencil; and a chain stitch for the details at the base of the eraser.

Cut out the pieces.

5. Cut out the embroidered motif in a 9" x 5" rectangle with the motif centered in the rectangle.

6. From the green fabric, cut:
   1 piece: 9" x 5"

   From the lining fabric, cut:
   2 pieces: 9" x 5"

Assemble the pouch.

7. Fold the top edge of each rectangle to the **Wrong** side by ¼" and press.

8. Separate the Velcro sides. Pin one side of it along the top edge of the **Right** side of one lining piece. Machine-sew around all of the edges of the tape, as close as you can to the edges. Repeat to sew the other side of the tape to the other lining piece.

9. Pin the lining pieces together, Right sides facing and raw edges even. Machine-sew around the sides and bottom edges. Clip the corners and press the seam allowances toward the center of the pouch.

10. Pin the outside pieces together, Right sides facing and raw edges even (make sure the top edges are still turned to the Wrong side). Machine-sew around the sides and bottom edges. Clip the corners and turn the pouch Right-side out. Press.

11. Put the lining piece inside the outside piece. Using a hand-sewing needle and thread, **slipstitch** the layers together.

P.S. Look up René Magritte. He actually started as a poster and advertisement designer for a wallpaper factory until he could support himself full-time with art.

WHERE YOU HANG OUT

Get your pad party-ready. The projects in this chapter are all about comfort for lounging around in your room. A cheery bean bag and cozy fleece throw, wild felt rug, dreamy lighting—it's all you need to set the scene. You could even host a Girls' Night In and make a few of the projects together. Then prepare yourself for serious hallway envy.

BYOC (Bring Your Own Craft!)

Hook up with like-minded friends and host your own craft night. Here are some tips to get your stitch on:

▸ Send an e-mail to gauge interest, determine skills, and set up an initial meeting.

▸ Create a Web page for your group where you can keep connected, share tips, and schedule get-togethers.

▸ Plan to meet regularly at the same time.

▸ Find a spot that gives you room to create, such as a café or the student lounge. For a small group, a dorm room works just fine.

▸ Make a list of favorite craft stores in the area to e-mail everyone before the meeting. Discuss who will bring what: yarn, fabric, thread, glue, how-to books and magazines, etc.

▸ Mix it up! Alternate meetings, from a lesson in knitting by a group expert (a scarf is a great beginner project) to a theme night (holidays always make great themes) to a casual craft night where anything goes.

▸ Bring a trash bag for easy cleanup! And keep hungry crafters satiated with plenty of treats.

▸ Take photos of completed projects to post on your site, or create a scrapbook to share with the group.

YOU'LL NEED:

▸ Zebra rug template

▸ 2 yards (72" wide) gray felt

▸ 2 yards (72" wide) orange felt

▸ 4 yards (72" wide) cream felt

▸ 6' x 2' piece of 2" grid pattern paper

▸ Carbon paper and tracing wheel

▸ Pencil

▸ Scissors

▸ Fabric glue

SKILL LEVEL **201**

Cut-It-Out Felt Rug

Non-fraying felt makes this project a cinch, and the zebra motif will have your hallmates demanding where you found it. It's so simple you can adjust the technique to make a rug in just about any size or style, including a welcome mat (or good-bye mat behind the door).

Make the pattern.

1. Using the zebra rug template, draw the zebra rug pattern onto the 2" grid pattern paper. Draw a 2" border around the edges and cut out the template around the outer edges.

Cut out the pieces.

2. Fold the gray felt in half lengthwise and lay it on the floor. Lay the template on the felt with the template's straight edge even with the fold in the fabric. Following the instructions on the carbon paper, trace the design onto the felt with the **tracing wheel**.

3. Remove the template and carbon paper. Pin the layers of felt together and cut out the design.

4. Repeat for the orange felt.

Assemble the rug.

5. Lay the cream felt out flat on the floor. Unfold the gray felt piece and lay it flat on top of the cream felt. Pin in place.

6. Cut the cream layer to the same size as the outer edge of the gray felt. Glue the layers together with fabric glue and let the glue dry.

7. Place the rug over the cream felt again and cut out another layer. Glue the layers together with fabric glue and let dry.

8. Flip the rug over and place the orange piece in place, matching the raw edges. Pin the layers in place and glue them together.

SKILL LEVEL **201**

YOU'LL NEED:

- Computer and inkjet printer
- 8 digital photos
- 10-pack of sew-in inkjet fabric sheets
- ½ yard (45" wide) cotton fabric in orange print
- ¼ yard (45" wide) cotton fabric in cream print
- ½ yard (45" wide) felt in brown
- 2 yards (½" wide) velvet ribbon in cream
- 1 large embroidery hoop (12" diameter)
- 8 medium embroidery hoops (6" diameter)
- 4 small embroidery hoops (3" diameter)
- Fabric chalk
- Glue gun and glue sticks
- Iron and ironing board
- Scissors

Embroidery-Hoop Photo Mobile

Conversation piece? We think so. Share family and friends with new pals simply by printing their photos on fabric! It's just the cure for those homesick blues.

Print the photos.

1. Following the manufacturer's instructions, print four 6" x 6" and four 3" x 3" digital photos onto the fabric sheets. Place them in four of the medium hoops (place the clasp at the bottom) and all of the small hoops (place the clasp at the top). Fold the edges of the fabric to the back of the hoop, trimming any excess fabric.

Cut the fabric.

2. Place the large hoop on the orange fabric. Cut the fabric 1½" around the hoop, then secure the fabric in the hoop. Repeat with two of the medium hoops.

3. Repeat step 2, using cream fabric and two of the medium hoops.

4. Using fabric chalk, trace a medium hoop 8 times and a small hoop 4 times on the brown felt. Cut the circles out along the trace lines.

Glue the fabric.

5. For all hoops, press the fabric's edges over to the back. Use the glue gun to glue the fabric flaps to the inside of the hoops.

6. Using the glue gun, glue the felt circles from step 4 to the back of the medium and small hoops, with the chalk side facing in.

Assemble the mobile.

7. Cut the velvet ribbon into quarters. Glue one end of each ribbon to the inside of the large hoop at the quadrant points.

8. Turn the large hoop upside down. Glue the clasp parts of four of the medium hoops (alternate cream and orange fabric) to the inside of the large hoop, at the opposite quadrant points from the ribbon. Let the glue dry.

9. Glue the remaining four medium hoops (with photos) to the bottoms of the medium hoops. The clasps will hang at the bottom when hung. Let the glue dry.

10. Glue the four small hoops to the bottom of the medium hoops, matching clasps.

11. Hang as desired by hanging from the four ribbons at the top.

Conversation Coasters

Would you rather go to class naked for a day or lose your teeth for a year? Tough question. Get to know new friends with these conversation-starting coasters. Put fortunes, horoscopes, or thought-provoking Would You Rather? questions and see how much (more) fun hanging with your hallmates can be.

Makes three 4"-diameter coasters.

Cut the fabric.

1. From one main piece of cotton, cut: 2 squares: 5" x 5"

   Place them **Right** sides together and trace the circle template on one **Wrong** side. Pin the squares together and trim ½" around circle.

2. From the coordinating cotton, cut: 2 squares: 3" x 3"

   Press a ½" fold along the length-wise side (the side meant to face the "mouth").

Stitch the fabric.

3. Stitch along trace line of the circle in step 1, leaving a 2" opening.
   Note: Handstitching these circles can be easier for a beginner sewer. When machine stitching, work slowly, turning the fabric occasionally (you may need to raise the **presser foot** at times; if so, keep the needle pierced into the fabric so you don't skip over the trace line).

4. Turn the coaster inside out, press, and hand-stitch it closed. Iron flat again.

Glue the mouth pieces.

5. Place the flat edge of the half-circle template on the Wrong side of the fabric from step 2, centered on the folded edge. Trim ½" from the curved edge.

6. With the iron on a low setting, press the fabric over the template's curved edge. Remove the template and press the curve again.

7. Place the half-circle piece on the circle piece, Wrong sides together, joining the curved edges and meeting the fold at the circle's midpoint.

8. Pin or **fingerpress** the half-circle's curved edge to the circle's curved edge. Glue them together along the curved edge only.

9. Repeat steps 5 to 8 with the other 3" square to close the mouth of your conversation coaster.
   Hint: It helps to tape the centers of the semicircles together when gluing the other side to make sure they match up.

Get the conversation started.

10. Write messages on 2" x 2" pieces of cardstock and place them inside the mouths.

YOU'LL NEED:

- Coaster templates 1 + 2
- ¼ yard (45" wide) cotton fabric
- ¼ yard (45" wide) coordinating cotton fabric
- Cardstock for the messages
- Fabric glue
- Sewing machine
- Iron and ironing board
- Stitch Kit (see page 14)

SKILL LEVEL 201

"WOULD YOU RATHER" IDEAS TO GET YOU STARTED:

Would you rather . . .

lose your voice or your eyesight?

marry a pirate or a penthouse owner?

gain 30 pounds or have to run 30 miles?

graduate in one year or six?

give up alcohol or sweets?

eat everything with your hands or drink everything through an eye dropper?

walk in on your parents having sex or have your parents walk in on you having sex?

fart audibly in class or noticeably wet your pants in class?

earn a million (dollars) or save a million (people)?

win an Oscar or a Nobel?

break up with your boyfriend or your best friend?

fail a class or live with your parents senior year?

go bald or grow an unwaxable mustache?

Felt Backgammon/ Checkers Board

Relieve boredom and brain-rot with a stow-away board game. For game pieces, you can paint bottle caps or cut out extra circles from the felt (both can also be used as chips for an impromptu poker night). Or paint symbols onto the pieces for an easy chess option.

Cut the pieces.

1 From the striped fabric, cut:
1 square: 18 ½" x 18 ½"

From the polka-dot fabric, cut:
1 square: 18 ½" x 18 ½"

2 From the double-sided fusible web, cut:
32 squares: 2 ¼" x 2 ¼"

Using a **press cloth**, fuse the squares onto the goldenrod felt. Cut out the pieces but do not peel off the paper backing yet.

3 Use the felt game template. From the double-sided fusible web, cut:
24 points

Using a press cloth, fuse 12 points onto the goldenrod felt and 12 points onto the gray felt. Cut out the pieces but do not peel off the paper backing yet.

Assemble the board.

4 Peel the paper backing off the points and arrange them onto the striped fabric square as shown in the photo. Fuse them in place using a press cloth. Cut an 18 ½" piece of **bias tape** and pin it in place across the center of the points. Machine-sew in place along both long edges of the tape.

5 Peel the paper backing off the felt squares and arrange them onto the polka-dot fabric square. Fuse the squares in place using a press cloth.

6 Pull apart the Velcro. Pin one side of the Velcro ½" away from one raw edge of the polka-dot fabric square on the **Wrong** side of the fabric. Pin the other side of the Velcro ½" away from one raw edge of the striped fabric square on the Wrong side of the fabric. Machine-sew the Velcro in place, sewing around all edges.

7 Cut two 18 ½" pieces of bias tape. Pin each one over the raw edge of each fabric square with Velcro. Sandwich the raw edge of the fabric inside the bias tape and machine-sew the tape in place, making sure you sew through the backside of the tape, as well.

8 Pin the two fabric squares together with Wrong sides facing, Velcro closed, and raw edges even. **Baste** around the raw edges through both layers using a ¼" **seam allowance**.

9 Pin the remaining bias tape around the raw edge of the game board, sandwiching the raw edges inside the bias tape. Stitch the tape in place along the inside folded edge, making sure you stitch through the backside of the bias tape at the same time. At each end of the bias tape, turn under ½" to hide the raw edge.

YOU'LL NEED:

- ‣ Felt game template
- ‣ ⅝ yard (45" wide) striped fabric
- ‣ ⅝ yard (45" wide) polka-dot fabric
- ‣ ¼ yard (72" wide) goldenrod felt
- ‣ ¼ yard (72" wide) gray felt
- ‣ 1 yard (22" wide) double-sided fusible web
- ‣ 3¼ yards (½" wide) double-fold **bias tape** in red
- ‣ 16" (½" wide) sew-in Velcro
- ‣ Sewing machine
- ‣ Iron and ironing board
- ‣ Stitch Kit (see page 14)

Better Bean Bag

Extra seating, an ottoman, beanbag, or end table—this bulbous cushion works overtime as so many things, which is exactly what you want in a small space. The patchwork style allows you to mix and match prints to coordinate with your roommate's colors.

Make the top.

(Use a ½" **seam allowance**.)

1 Use the tufted floor cushion template. From each of the six top fabrics, cut: 1 wedge

2 Pin two top pieces together with **Right** sides facing and the raw edges even. Sew along one long edge and press the seam allowance open.

3 Repeat to sew all the pieces together to assemble the top.

Make the sides.

4 From the side fabric, cut: 2 pieces: 60 ½" long x 20" wide

5 Pin the two pieces together with Right sides facing and the 20" edges even. Machine-sew along one 20" side.

6 Pin the two pieces together with Right sides facing and raw edges even along the remaining 20" edges. Machine-sew.

7 Pin the sides to the assembled top piece with Right sides facing and raw edges even. Sew together on the machine. Press the seam allowance toward the assembled top piece.

Make the bottom.

8 Cut a 38" diameter circle from the bottom fabric.

9 Pin the remaining raw edge of the sides to the bottom piece with Right sides facing and raw edges even. Machine-sew, leaving a 5" opening. Press the seam allowance toward the assembled top piece.

Stuff and tuft.

10 Pour Poly-Fil bean bag filler into the cushion until it is as full as you want it. **Slipstitch** the opening closed (or you can glue it shut).

11 Following the manufacturer's instructions, cover the buttons with fabric.

12 If you want to tuft the cushion, thread the upholstery needle with two strands of button thread and push it through the center of your cushion, leaving a 10" to 12" tail. Pass the needle through the shank of one button, then, going through the same hole in the top, pass the needle back through the cushion and through the shank of the second button on the bottom of the cushion. Remove the needle and tie the thread ends together, pulling the thread taught. Tie the threads together again around the button shank and cut off the excess.

If you don't want to tuft the cushion, simply sew the covered button at the center of the top and the center of the bottom for a finishing touch.

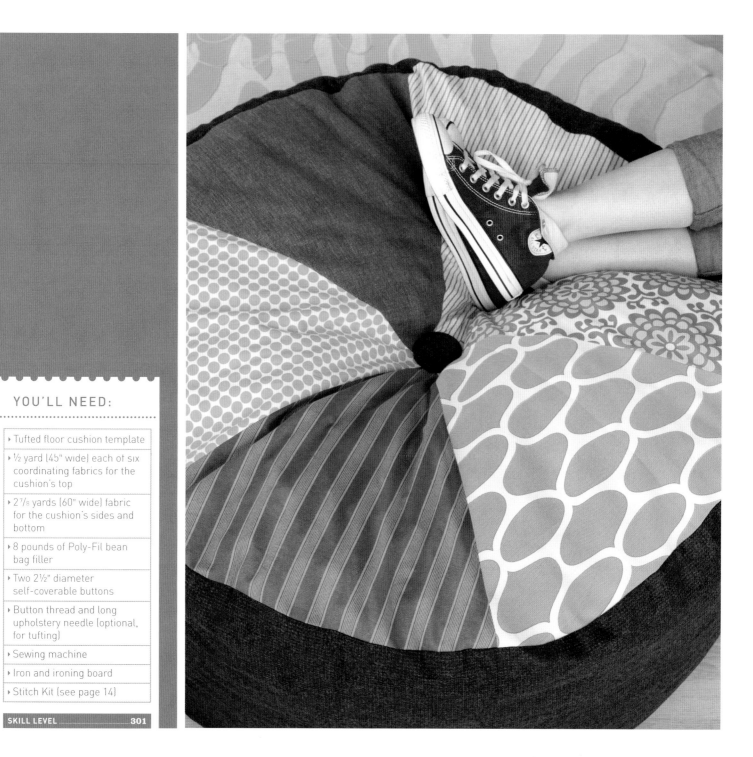

Paint-inside-the-Lines Lantern

A kindergartner's favorite pastime, painting inside the lines gets a grown-up makeover with Chinese paper lanterns and a fresh, edgy design. Light as a feather, these lanterns are easy to hang with minimal effort.

Transfer the design.

1. Enlarge the template to fit your lantern. Tape the template to the inside of the lantern. (To make sure the tape won't rip the paper when you remove it, first stick the tape to the back of your hand so that the oils from your skin take away some of the stickiness.)

2. Draw the outline of the template onto the lantern using a dull pencil.

Paint the design.

3. Using a paintbrush and paint, fill in the design. Let the paint dry and go over the outlines with black marker, adding details.

P.S. In China, paper lanterns come in various sizes and shapes and therefore have many names. This shape is called the Tomato Light or Big Red. Traditionally red, these lanterns also used to adorn the brothels (hence the "red light district").

Draft Snake

Dorms not only leave a bit to be desired aesthetically, they can also leave a draft. Sometimes you won't have control over the temperature, and space heaters are often not allowed, so have this little guy on hand to keep your place warm and toasty.

Measure the width of your window or doorway.

(Use a ½" **seam allowance**.)

1 You want your draft snake to be the same size. Our window was 36" wide. Use more fabric for more width.

Cut out the pieces.

2 Determine the finished length of your fabric pieces so that when they are all stitched together they will be the same length found in step 1. We made our solid piece 14" long, the hounds-tooth piece 6 ½" long, the green print piece 6 ½" long, and the striped piece 9" long.

3 To determine the size of all the pieces that you will cut out, add 1" to all of the lengths found in step 2. The width of all of the pieces will be 10".

Assemble the pieces.

4 Pin two pieces together along the 10" edge with their **Right** sides facing. Machine-sew the 10" edge.

5 Repeat so that all of the pieces are sewn together.

Finish the snake.

6 Fold the snake in half with the Right sides facing and the long edges even. Sew around all of the edges, leaving a 2" opening.

7 Clip the corners and turn the snake Right-side out. Fill with your choice of filling, and **slipstitch** or glue the opening shut.

Argyle Fleece Throw

This low-sew throw gives new meaning to the phrase "college sweater vest." Preppy, yes, but the diamond-shaped pattern feels less stuffy in these vibrant colors. It's super-easy with basic stitching, keeps you warm on winter nights, and makes the perfect picnic blanket!

Cut out the pieces.

1. From the cream fleece, cut:
1 piece: 54" x 70"

   From the goldenrod fleece, cut:
1 piece: 58" x 74"

Create the pattern.

2. Following the diagram, draw a diamond using the same measurements on the paper. Cut out the diamond and use it as a template to draw onto the cream fleece in rows. The points of the diamonds should be touching. Don't worry about getting it exact.

3. Cut out every other row of diamonds ¼" inside of the marked lines.

Stitch out the pattern.

4. Lay the cream fleece over the goldenrod fleece and pin in place. Using the yardstick and marker, draw lines through the centers of the diamonds at an angle as pictured to create the argyle pattern.

5. Thread the embroidery needle with six strands of embroidery floss. Stitch out the lines and outlines of all the diamonds with a running stitch (see page 19), securing the two layers of fleece together.

Make the border.

6. Fold the edges of the goldenrod piece toward the cream piece and pin in place. Stitch the goldenrod fleece down using a blanket stitch (see page19).

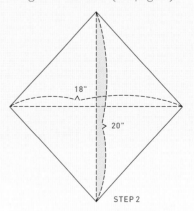

18"

20"

STEP 2

YOU'LL NEED:

- 2⅛ yards (60" wide) cream fleece
- 2⅛ yards (60" wide) golden-rod fleece
- 15 skeins of embroidery floss in cranberry
- Large-eye embroidery needle
- Water-soluble marker
- Paper
- Pencil
- Scissors
- Pins
- Yardstick

WHERE YOU WASH

Welcome to the world of communal bathrooms. Sure, sharing with your brother was bad, but fifteen girls? Not to worry. We've got just the icebreakers for those over-the-sink chats: "How cool is that tote?" "Love the slippers!" To which you proudly reply, "I made it myself."

YOU'LL NEED:

· Laundry bag base template

· 1⅛ yard (45" wide) cotton fabric for the bottom half of the bag

· 1⅞ yards (45" wide) cotton fabric for the top section of the bag

· ⅓ yards (45" wide) contrasting cotton fabric for the pocket and drawstring

· 8½" x 12¾" remnant of fusible **interfacing**

· 2½ yards (1½" wide) **webbing** for the straps

· 2 yards (¼" wide) cording for the drawstring

· 6½" (⅝" wide) sew-in Velcro

· 1 (⅝" diameter) heavy-duty snap

· 4 (1½" wide) D-rings

· Safety pin

· Sewing machine

· Iron and ironing board

· Stitch Kit (see page 14)

SKILL LEVEL 401

Laundry Day Backpack

Laundry day will always be boring, but this super-functional backpack (no more sling over the shoulder hunchback-style!) makes it easy. The Velcro pouch keeps quarters secure, and a snappable strap holds on to your detergent. If only it could clean your dirty clothes.

Cut the pieces.

1 From the bottom fabric, cut:
1 base piece (using the laundry bag base template)
template, cut the following:
1 piece: 19 ½" x 10"
1 piece: 37 ½" x 10"
1 detergent strap: 4 ¼" x 12 ¾"

From the top fabric, cut:
1 piece: 19 ½" x 19 ¾"
1 piece: 37 ½" x 19 ¾"

2 From the contrasting fabric, cut:
1 pocket: 8" x 7"
2 drawstring casings: 3 ½" x 28 ¾"

From the **interfacing**, cut:
2 detergent straps: 4 ¼" x 12 ¾"

3 Pin the two drawstring casing pieces together along one 3 ½" edge, **Wrong** sides facing, then sew along that edge using a ¾" **seam allowance**. Trim and **topstitch** the seam to create **flat-felled seams**.

Sew the bottom of the backpack.

4 With the Wrong sides together, pin the 10" edges of the 19 ½" x 10" piece of bottom fabric to the 10" edges of the 37 ½" x 10" piece of bottom fabric. Sew together using a ¾" seam allowance. Trim and topstitch the seam to create flat-felled seams.

5 Pin the sewn bottom pieces to the base piece with the Wrong sides facing, matching the seams of the bottom pieces with the corners of the base piece. Sew together using a ¾" seam allowance. Trim and topstitch the seam to create a flat-felled seam.

Sew the pocket and detergent strap.

6 Fold both 7" edges and one 8" edge of the pocket to the Wrong side ¼" twice and press. Topstitch in place along the inside folded edges.

7 Fold the remaining 8" edge of the pocket to the Wrong side ½" and press. Pull apart the Velcro and pin the hook side on the Wrong side of the pocket, centered on the raw edge. Machine-sew around the edges of the hook tape.

continued

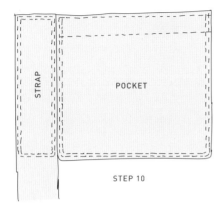

STRAP

POCKET

STEP 10

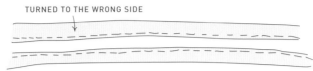

TURNED TO THE WRONG SIDE

STEP 15

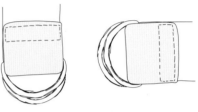

STEP 18

8 Following the manufacturer's instructions, fuse one piece of interfacing to the Wrong side of the detergent strap piece. Fuse the second interfacing piece over the previous one. Fold the detergent strap in half with **Right** sides facing, matching the 12 ¾" sides. Stitch with a ¼" seam allowance around the edges, leaving one short end open. Trim the corners and turn the strap Right-side out. Press and **slipstitch** the opening shut.

Sew the top of the backpack.

9 Position the pocket and detergent strap centered on the 37 ½" x 19 ¾" piece of top fabric. With fabric chalk, mark where the top edge of the pocket is. Remove the pocket and

the detergent strap. Sew the loop side of the Velcro where the pocket's top edge was on the fabric, sewing around all of the edges of the tape.

10 Position the pocket and detergent strap pack on the fabric and pin in place. Sew in place around the sides and bottom edges of the pocket and the sides and center of the detergent strap that are even with the pocket. Leave the bottom half of the detergent strap unstitched as shown in the illustration. Stitch the detergent strap again inside the previous stitching lines.

11 Following the manufacturer's instructions, attach each snap piece on either end of the detergent strap.

12 Pin the 19 ¾" edges of the top piece together with the Right sides facing to form a tube. Sew the seams with a ¾" seam allowance. Trim and topstitch both seams to create flat-felled seams.

Finish the backpack body.

13 Pin the top half of the backpack to the bottom half of the backpack with the Wrong sides facing and raw edges even. Sew with a ¾" seam allowance. Trim and topstitch the seam to create a flat-felled seam.

14 Fold the top edge of the backpack to the Wrong side ½" and press. Fold the top edge of the backpack to the Wrong side 1 ½" and press. Topstitch in place along the inner folded edge.

STEP 20

15 Fold all edges of the drawstring casing to the Wrong side ½" twice and press. Topstitch in place close to the inner folded edges as shown in the illustration.

16 Pin the drawstring casing to the backpack ¾" below the top edge of the backpack. The short ends (where the drawstring will come out) should be centered over the pocket and detergent strap. Topstitch in place along the top and bottom of the casing, leaving the short ends unstitched.

Add the straps.

17 Cut the **webbing** into four equal pieces.

18 Lace two D-rings onto one piece of webbing. Press one end of the webbing under ½". Fold the same end under 1". Push the D-rings down to the folded end. Sew in place, as pictured in the illustration, in a rectangle. Repeat for another piece of webbing and the remaining two D-rings.

19 Fold one end of a remaining piece of webbing under 1½" twice and press. Topstitch the folded edge in place around the edges of the folds in the shape of a square. Stitch from corner to corner across the center of the square, creating a stitched "X" within the square. Repeat for the remaining piece of webbing.

20 Press the raw ends of the webbing pieces to the Wrong side ½". Position the unstitched edges of the webbing pieces centered on the back of the backpack 9" apart horizontally. The pieces with the D-rings should be the top two straps. Make sure that the folded-under raw ends are face-down on the backpack, and pin them in place. Stitch in place on each piece of webbing in a 1½" square. Stitch across the centers of each square from corner to corner to create an "X" in each square as shown in the illustration.

21 Pierce the safety pin into one end of the cording and close the pin. Push the pin through the drawstring casing to get the cording all the way through. Remove the safety pin. Knot each end of the cord to finish.

Toiletry Tote

Iron-on vinyl helps you turn your favorite cottons into water-resistant fabric, which makes this awesome tote shower-safe. Just keep in mind that it's water-resistant, not waterproof, so avoid putting it directly under the shower stream.

Cut out the pieces.

(Use a ½" **seam allowance**.)

1 From the outside fabric, cut:
2 pieces: 10" x 7"
2 pieces: 7" x 7"

From the lining fabric, cut:
3 pieces: 10" x 7"
2 pieces: 7" x 7"

From the fusible vinyl, cut:
5 pieces: 10" x 7"
4 pieces: 7" x 7"

Fuse the vinyl.

2 Following the manufacturer's instructions, fuse each fusible vinyl piece onto a piece of fabric of equal size cut in step 1. Save the paper backings.

Assemble the pieces.

3 Pin one 10" x 7" piece of the outer fabric to a coordinated 7" x 7" piece along one 7" edge with **Right** sides facing. Machine-sew together. Press the seam allowance open using the vinyl paper backing saved from step 2.

4 Pin the second 7" x 7" piece of the outer fabric to the remaining 7" edge of the sewn 10" x 7" piece with Right sides facing. Machine-sew together. Press the seam allowance open using the vinyl paper backing saved from step 2.

5 Pin the remaining 10" x 7" to one 7" raw edge of the assembled piece with Right sides facing. Machine-sew together. Press the seam allowance open using the vinyl paper backing saved from step 2.

6 Pin the two remaining 7" raw edges of the outer edge pieces together with Right sides facing. Machine-sew together. Press the seam allowance open using the vinyl paper backing saved from step 2.

7 Assemble the lining pieces using the same method.

8 Pin the assembled outer piece to the assembled lining piece along their top edges with Right sides facing. Machine-sew together along the top edge and turn the pieces Right side out.

Insert the cardboard.

9 Pin the layers of the tote together along the corner seams. Sew the layers together along each corner seam, securing the lining to the outer fabric at each corner.

10 Insert a piece of cardboard between the outer and lining fabrics on each side of the tote.

Assemble the bottom.

11 Glue the remaining lining piece onto one side of the remaining cardboard piece. Turn the tote upside down on your work surface. **Fingerpress** all of the bottom seam allowance toward the outside of the tote.

12 Place the bottom piece over the bottom of the tote, making sure all of the seam allowances are turned toward the outside and the lining side of the bottom piece is facedown. Glue in place.

13 Turn the seam allowances on the bottom edge toward the bottom of the tote and fingerpress in place. Glue to secure all seam allowances down.

14 Place the last vinyl piece over the bottom, hiding all seam allowances. Trim to fit and glue in place.

Finish the tote.

15 Seal all of the seams with a thin layer of glue. Let dry.

16 Hand-sew the **webbing** to the bag at the center of each side, about 1" below the top edge.

17 Hand-sew a button on each strap as pictured.

YOU'LL NEED:

- ¼ yard (45" wide) cotton fabric for the outside of the tote
- ¼ yard (45" wide) cotton fabric for the lining of the tote
- 1 yard (17" wide) iron-on vinyl in matte
- 1 (6½" x 9") piece of vinyl for the bottom of the tote
- ½ yard (1½" wide) **webbing**
- Two 1" diameter buttons
- 3 (8½" x 6") pieces of cardboard
- 2 (6" x 6") pieces of cardboard
- Krazy Glue
- Sewing machine
- Iron and ironing board
- Stitch Kit (see page 14)

SKILL LEVEL   401

Fuzzy Slippers

Accessorize down to your tippy toes with fuzzy slippers—they're certain to keep your feet happy. Not a fan of faux fur? Try cushy fleece or another of your favorite fabrics instead.

For tips on making your own bias tape like we did, turn to page 21!

Cut out the pieces.

1. Use a photocopier to enlarge the templates to the right size for your feet. From the **batting**, cut:

4 soles

2 straps (1 in reverse)

From the fur, cut:

2 soles (1 in reverse)

From the vinyl, cut:

2 soles (1 in reverse)

From the cotton, cut:

2 straps (1 in reverse)

From the strap-lining fabric, cut:

2 straps (1 in reverse)

From the tear-away stabilizer, cut:

4 pieces: 6" x 12"

Assemble the sole.

2. Lay one piece of stabilizer out on your work surface. Lay one vinyl sole on top of the stabilizer, with the **Right** side facedown. Layer two batting sole pieces over the vinyl, then a fur sole piece on the top. Make sure all of the sole pieces are facing the same direction. Lay a second piece of tear-away stabilizer on the top. Pin through all layers.

3. Sew around the edge with a ¼" **seam allowance**, securing all of the layers together. Tear away the stabilizer from the sole's top side.

4. Repeat for the second sole.

Make the strap.

5. Lay one strap piece of batting on your work surface. Lay one strap-lining piece on the batting, Right-side up. Lay the coordinating cotton strap piece on the top, Right-side up. Pin through all layers, making sure all raw edges are even.

6. Sew the top and bottom edge of the strap layers together using a ½" seam allowance. Turn the strap Right-side out, sandwiching the batting in the center.

7. Sew the side edges together, using a ½" seam allowance.

8. Repeat to make the second strap.

9. Pin the strap approximately 2 ½" below the toe, with the strap's raw edges even with the sole's raw edges.

10. Stitch all layers together along the side seam with a ½" seam allowance.

11. Repeat to attach the second strap.

Finish the slippers.

12. Pin double-folded **bias tape** around the slipper edges, turning under the raw edges of the tape. **Edgestitch** the tape in place close to the inside edge of the tape.

13. Tear away the stabilizer from the back of the slipper.

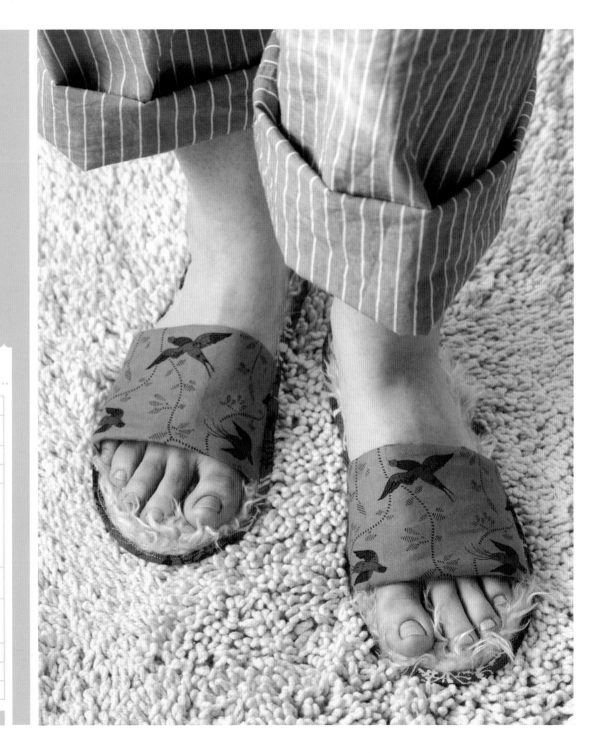

YOU'LL NEED:

‣ Slippers templates 1 + 2

‣ 24" x 24" remnant of extra-loft **batting**

‣ ⅓ yard (60" wide) faux fur

‣ ⅓ yard (60" wide) vinyl

‣ ¼ yard (45" wide) cotton fabric for the flap (you can use this for the inside of the strap, too, or get a second ¼ yard (45" wide) piece for the backside)

‣ 1 package of tear-away stabilizer

‣ Enough ½" wide double-fold **bias tape** to go around your shoe template twice

‣ Sewing machine

‣ Iron and ironing board

‣ Stitch Kit (see page 14)

Fleece Robe

Maybe you pulled an all-nighter or simply can't be bothered to get dressed. Thanks to this cuddly all-day robe, you don't have to. And since it has a hood to boot, you can keep your bad hair days under wraps!

Make the pattern.

(Use a ½" **seam allowance** unless otherwise noted.)

1 On pattern paper, draw out your pattern pieces using the robe measurements on page 121. From the body's fleece, cut:

1 back (cut on the fold)

2 hoods

2 fronts

2 sleeves

2 From the other fleece, cut:

4 belt loops: 7" x 1"

2 **binding** pieces: 46½" x 2"

2 belts: 58" x 3"

4 pockets: 6" x 7"

Attach the pockets.

3 Pin two pocket pieces together with raw edges even and **Wrong** sides facing. Sew around all of the edges with a ¼" seam allowance. Repeat for the second pocket.

4 Pin one pocket to one robe front with the bottom edge 14" from the bottom **hem**, and the outermost corner 4" from the side edge. Sew the pocket onto the robe. Repeat for the second pocket on the other side.

Sew the shoulder seams.

5 Pin one robe front to the robe back with the shoulder edges even and the **Right** sides facing. Sew the shoulder seam as shown in the illustration.

STEP 5

STEP 7

6 Repeat for the second front piece.

Make the hood.

7 Pin the two hood pieces together with their Right sides facing and raw edges even. Sew along the curved edge as shown in the illustration.

continued

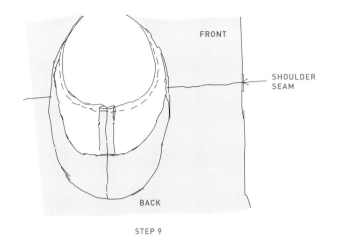

FRONT

SHOULDER
SEAM

BACK

STEP 9

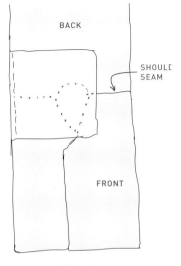

BACK

SHOULDER
SEAM

FRONT

STEP 10

Attach the hood.

8 Pin the hood to the robe with Right sides facing and the seam in the hood even with the center back of the robe. The edge of the hood will extend past the shoulder seams on the robe.

9 Sew the hood to the robe along the raw edges as shown in the illustration. Make sure to not bunch up the fabric as it feeds into the machine. **Finger-press** the seam allowance toward the hood.

Attach the sleeves.

10 Pin one sleeve in place with the center of one 19" edge even with the shoulder seam as shown in the illustration. Sew in place and fingerpress the seam allowance toward the robe. Repeat with the second sleeve.

Make the belt loops.

11 Pin two belt loop pieces together with the Wrong sides facing and raw edges even. Sew the pieces together with a ¼" seam allowance. Repeat to make the second loop.

12 Fold one belt loop in half, matching the 1" edges. Sew the 1" raw edges together on the machine with a ¼" seam allowance.

13 Pin a belt loop to the Right side of one robe front with the loop's raw edge even with the robe's raw side edge. Place the belt loop 20" above the robe's hem. Sew in place.

14 Repeat for the second belt loop.

Sew the side seams.

15 Pin the robe together as shown in the illustration with Right-sides facing and the side edges even.

16 Sew the arm and side seams on the machine.

Turn the robe Right-side out to finish it.

17 Trim the top corner on each robe front, to smooth out the corners.

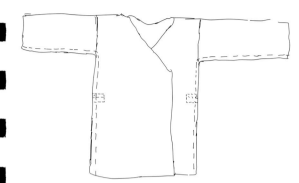

STEP 15

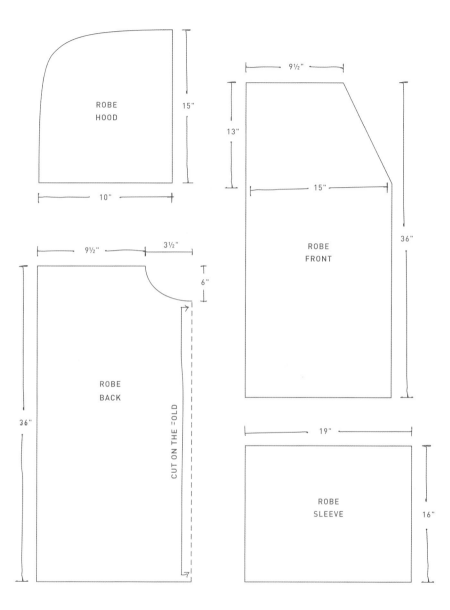

ROBE HOOD

15"

10"

ROBE BACK

36"

CUT ON THE FOLD

9½" 3½"

6"

ROBE FRONT

9½"

13"

15"

36"

ROBE SLEEVE

19"

16"

18 Pin the two binding pieces together with the Right sides facing and one 2" edge even. Sew together and finger-press the seam allowance open

19 Pin the binding to the robe along the inner edge of the robe with the Right side of the robe facing the Wrong side of the binding.

20 Sew the binding to the robe on the machine ½" inside its raw edges.

Make the belt.

21 Pin the two belt pieces together with the Wrong sides facing and raw edges even. Sew around the edges on the machine ½" inside all of the edges.

Embellished Towels

Give plain towels a personal touch with trims and appliqué. Keep in mind that you'll wash your towels often, so use washable fabrics and trims and prewash them before stitching. For a cool monogram, check out the Monogram Sham instructions on page 36.

Apply the appliqué.

1. Using fabric chalk, trace the desired template onto the appliqué fabric. Cut out the appliqué.

2. Pin the appliqué to the towel. Cut two pieces of stabilizer and put one behind the design and one on top of it.

3. Sew the design onto the towel using a **zigzag stitch**.

4. Tear or wash away the stabilizer.

Make the ruffle.

5. Measure how long and wide you would like your ruffle. Double the length and add 1" to the width.

6. Fold the top and bottom edge of the ruffle to the **Wrong** side ¼" and press. Repeat to hide the raw edge and **edgestitch** in place.

7. On the machine, **baste** along the top edge of the ruffle, backstitching at one end. Repeat to make a second row just below that one.

8. Pull the **bobbin** threads on the side that doesn't have backstitching to gather the fabric into a ruffle. Once it's the right size, knot the threads.

9. Sew the ruffle to your towel on the machine using a traditional stitch close to the top edge.

10. Remove the basting stitches with a seam ripper.

P.S. It's a good idea to put a second layer of stabilizer on top of the towel while you're sewing to tame those fuzzy bits

YOU'LL NEED:

- Towel templates 1 + 2
- 1 towel
- Fabric for appliqués
- Fabric for ruffles (twice as long as your finished ruffle)
- Tear-away or wash-away stabilizer
- Trims
- Fabric glue
- Sewing machine
- Iron and ironing board
- Stitch Kit (see page 14)

SKILL LEVEL 301

Fabric Care Guide

Wash It Well

You want to wash all fabrics, trims, and embellished items before sewing, to avoid them puckering and shrinking after you've sewn them together. Iron as you go and your projects will look much more polished, too (see our ironing chart on page 126 for tips!). Okay, before we start sounding like a mother hen, here is a general chart to guide you through caring for new fabrics. (One more thing! Check the bolt at the store to ensure proper care.)

Batting: You don't need to preshrink or press batting.

Brocade: Pretty, isn't it? If you want it to stay that way, don't wash it. While you can wash brocade fabrics, they'll lose their sheen in the wash. Stick with the dry cleaners, or test a sample first in the washing machine.

Canvas: Washing canvas can give it a softer hand, but it will shrink. Make sure you have enough fabric to accommodate the shrinkage.

Chenille: Machine or hand-wash on the gentle cycle. Lay out flat to dry.

Corduroy: Wash in warm water and dry on a gentle cycle. You can fluff up tired corduroy by throwing it into the dryer with a damp towel for 10 to 15 minutes. When sewing, finish the raw edge with pinking shears to avoid a fraying, wrinkly mess.

Cotton: Cotton is very durable and can usually be washed repeatedly. It will shrink in hot-temperature washing and drying, however. If you have a delicate cotton, like a batiste, stick with hand-washing and line drying. When cutting, don't be afraid to snip and rip. Cottons are very forgiving and will rip along a straight grain with one forward snip.

Damask: Similar to brocade, except it looks the same on both sides. Wash in warm water and dry in the dryer on regular temperature.

Denim: Unless you want your whites blue, wash denim separately in warm water and dry at a regular temperature. It's a good idea to wash and dry denim twice before you begin your project because it tends to shrink a second time around.

Faux fur: Check the fabric bolt because some of these are actually washable in cold water. Dry them on the no-heat cycle or air dry.

Felt: Machine wash in warm water and tumble dry. Felt shrinks a lot and the colors may bleed, so allow for shrinkage when purchasing yardage and wash with like colors.

Flannel: Wash in hot water and dry on hot. This fabric will shrink considerably.

Fleece: Wash on the cool, gentle cycle and dry on a low setting. Do not dry clean.

Lace: Many laces are actually washable, so check the bolt. Hand-wash in warm water and air dry.

Leather: Leather cleaners work best on real leather. If you're dealing with pleather, check the label. You may be able to wash, dry-clean, or just wipe it clean with a damp rag (it all depends on the plastics used to create it).

Polyester: Machine wash on a warm cycle and line dry. You can dry it in the dryer on a low setting, but it causes a lot of static electricity.

Satin: Usually you can prewash satin in warm water and air dry.

Silk: Most silks can be hand-washed in cool water with a mild detergent and then air dried, but don't ever use bleach. Some silks are dry clean only, so check the bolt.

Suede: Most suedes can be hand-washed in lukewarm water and line dried. If you use a dryer, pull the suede out before it's completely dry and lay out flat.

Vinyl: No preshrinking necessary. You can clean it with a wipe of a damp cloth.

Wool: Many wools can be washed on a cool, gentle cycle, but will felt and shrink considerably if washed and dried on a high temperature.

Out Dang Spot!

You're bound to make a spill or two (or three) during your college days—and Mom won't be there to get the stain out. Here are some tips to keep your fabrics looking like new.

Beer: (and vodka, whiskey, you know): For washable fabrics, presoak in cold water and then wash in soapy water.

Blood: For a small amount, you can actually spot-treat with your own spit (sounds gross, but hey, it's your blood). For larger stains, rinse with cold water and then soak in a solution of 3 tablespoons ammonia to 1 gallon cool water for about an hour. Then wash as normal.

Candle wax: While candles are usually prohibited in dorms, it's still good to know. Let the wax cool and remove with a dull knife. Place a paper towel on either side of the stain and press with a warm iron. Wash away any color stains with soap and baking soda in hot water.

Chewing gum: Apply ice until the gum hardens and then scrape the gum off with a knife. Next, soak the stain in a mixture of water and liquid detergent.

Chocolate: Soak the stain in a mixture of 4 tablespoons borax and 2 ½ cups warm water.

Coffee or tea: Stretch the fabric over a bowl. Pour boiling water (use your coffeemaker or hot pot) through the stain from a height of about three feet. If the coffee had milk in it, spray with a stain remover first.

Grass: Rub the stain with detergent. You can also try a mixture of 1 part alcohol to 2 parts water and let it sit for 15 minutes.

Meet the Press

As you work on a project, it's important to iron as you go. This might seem tedious and annoying, but it will really help you end up with a nice finished project.

We've compiled a handy chart for reference in case your iron has more than just an on/off switch. This info is great when you're ironing your clothes, too.

Note: A **press cloth** is a cloth that you put over your fabric to protect it from direct contact with the iron. You can find a press cloth at any sewing store, or you can use a scrap of cotton fabric or old cotton shirt.

FABRIC	IRON SETTING
Acetate, Acrylic	Turn to the lowest setting on the iron, don't apply any extra pressure, and always iron from the **Wrong** side to avoid making shiny spots.
Cotton, Linen	You can use the highest setting and lots of steam for this stuff. If you see a shine coming, try using a press cloth.
Nylon	Don't use steam if you can help it, and keep to low heat settings—this stuff melts. Always iron on the Wrong side.
Polyester	Keep to a medium setting with a little bit of steam. Polyester can melt a little and get shiny, so press on the Wrong side.
Rayon	Use medium heat and always use a press cloth on the Wrong side of the fabric.
Silk	Set to a low heat setting and use a press cloth. You can use steam on heavier silks, but be careful about causing water spots on the fabric (some times they won't come out).
Wool	Low heat setting with heavy steam.

Grease: Try Murphy Oil Soap.

Ink: Treat polyester fabric with hair spray. Other fabrics can be spot-treated with rubbing alcohol, saturated with soap, and then washed.

Lipstick: Rub with white vinegar and rinse. Stain sticks also usually work for this.

Liquid makeup or mascara: Spot-treat with enzyme paste or a stain stick, then wash normally.

Nail polish: Rub in acetone polish remover from the underside with a paper towel. This may stain, so spot-check beforehand.

Sweat: Soak the stain in salt water for one hour. Next, rub a half-and-half solution of white vinegar and water on the stain. Rinse well and wash.

Tomato sauce: Soak in cool water for about half an hour. Apply a stain remover and rinse. Then apply an enzyme paste and rinse. Then apply clear vinegar and rinse.

Vomit (we've been there): Put a few drops of ammonia in about a cup of liquid detergent. Rub the solution into the stain, let it soak for 30 minutes, and rinse. Sponge a solution of ¼ cup salt to 2 quarts water onto the stain and let sit for 15 minutes. Rinse out the solution with water, and wash normally.

Wine: For white and red wines, soak the area with sparkling water as soon as you can. Pour salt over the stain and then stretch it over a bowl. From a height of about a foot, pour boiling water through the stain.

SOURCES:

More Fabric Savvy by Sandra Betzina. Newtown, CT: Taunton Press, 2005

The Super Stain Remover Book by Jack Cassimates. New York: Sterling Publishing, 1996

Resources

A.C. Moore
www.acmoore.com

Blick Art Materials
www.dickblick.com

Britex Fabrics
146 Geary Street
San Francisco, CA 94108
(415) 392-2910

Discount Fabrics
201 11th Street
San Francisco, CA 94103
(415) 495.4201

Hancock Fabrics
www.hancockfabrics.com

Hobby Lobby
www.hobbylobby.com

Home Depot
www.homedepot.com

IKEA
www.ikea.com

Jo-Ann Fabric and Craft Stores
www.joann.com

Michaels
www.michaels.com

Mood Fabrics
225 W. 37th Street, 3rd Floor
New York, NY 10018
www.moodfabrics.com

Pearl Paint
www.pearlpaint.com

Purl Patchwork
147 Sullivan Street
New York, NY 10012
(212) 420-8798
www.purlsoho.com

ReproDepot Fabrics
www.reprodepotfabrics.com

Satin Moon Fabrics
32 Clement Street
San Francisco, CA 94118
(415) 668-1623

Sew Mama Sew
www.sewmamasew.com

Sis Boom Fabrics
www.sisboom.com

Acknowledgments

Theresa: I would like to dedicate this book to my crafty sister, Kristen, who graduates from college the year this book is published. I would also like to thank my family and friends on both coasts for their support during the making of this book. Thanks to Diane Love for driving me all over the tri-state area for supplies with six-month-old Leo in tow.

Nicole: I would not have been able to finish this amazing project without the love and support of my family and friends. Every word of encouragement and act from loading the car for photoshoots to cutting out pieces I just didn't have time to finish myself was immensely appreciated. I cannot thank you enough.

From both of us: We would like to extend a special thanks to our editor Kate Prouty for her creative and editorial input as well as her enthusiastic support and encouragement. We would also like to thank the rest of the Chronicle Books creative team, including Jay Peter Salvas, Doug Ogan, Carleigh Bell, Yolanda Accinelli, and Sara Lorimer. Thanks also to Evan Sklar and Rizwan Alvi for making the shooting of this book not only fun but drama-free as well. We also appreciate the contributions from fabric designer Amy Butler, fabric suppliers Westminster Fibers and Moda Fabrics, and craft makers June Tailor, Dritz, Therm-O-Web, Wrights, and Darice.

Glossary

Appliqué: A decorative technique of sewing a piece of fabric on top of another. Can be done by hand or machine.

Backing: A fabric or stabilizer joined to the back of a fabric to hold in place.

Basting: A long stitch made by either the machine or by hand. Usually a temporary stitch.

Batting: A layer of stuffing that has been compressed into yardage for layering in quilts. These are sold by loft (or height) in a variety of fibers including polyester, cotton, cashmere, and wool.

Bias: The diagonal direction of a piece of fabric (45 degrees from the selvage).

Bias tape: *See* Binding.

Binding: A strip encasing a raw edge. Can be decorative or functional, and is usually made from a bias strip (also called bias tape).

Bobbin: A small spool that holds the lower thread on a sewing machine. These come in various sizes and in metal or plastic. Be sure to always buy the correct size for your machine.

Buckram: A very stiff fabric typically made of cotton or linen. Usually used as a reinforcement.

Cording foot: A presser foot for the machine designed to aid in stitching close to a cord. Also called a zipper foot.

Crosswise grain: The direction on the fabric running from selvage to selvage.

Edgestitch: Topstitching placed very close to an edge or fold.

Feed dogs: The part of the machine that feeds the fabric inside the plate below the presser foot.

Felt square: This is craft felt sold off the bolt. The standard size is 9" x 12".

Fingerpress: Pressing an area with your fingers to set a crease in place.

Flange: The lip on cording or welting. Usually used to fit into a seam.

Flat-felled seam: A strong seam that doesn't have any raw edges.

Grainline: The line that follows a fabric's selvage.

Grosgrain ribbon: Ribbon with horizontal grooves in it.

Hand-tack: To hand-sew in place with a few stitches in the same location.

Hem: Usually the finished bottom edge of a garment or drapery.

Interfacing: Comes in a variety of fibers and weights , this "stability" fabric helps you add shape to your project.

Lengthwise grain: The direction of fabric running along the selvage.

Miter: Diagonal seaming at a corner.

Nap: A brushed, raised, or textured surface that lies smoothly in one direction.

Pinking shears: Scissors that cut a zigzag into fabric, slowing down fraying.

Pivot: Stitching a corner by sewing up to it, leaving the needle in the fabric, raising the presser foot, and pivoting the fabric to make the turn.

Piping: Fabric-covered cord, used as a trim.

Preshrink: To wash and dry a piece of fabric or trim before you begin a project.

Press cloth: A piece of fabric placed over your project to prevent scorching when ironing.

Presser foot: The part of the sewing machine that presses down on the fabric so that the feed dogs will be able to pull the fabric through the machine. Never sew without lowering the presser foot. There are a wide variety of presser feet including buttonhole, zipper, zigzag, and cording.

Repeat: Printed fabrics will have a repeat in the print (where the print starts over again).

Right: The side of the fabric you want shown in the finished project. If the fabric is printed, it's the side where the print is brightest and clearest.

Seam allowance: The amount of space between the seam line and the raw edge of the fabric.

Selvage: The finished edge of the fabric, running lengthwise.

Slipstitch: An almost invisible stitch, simply slide needle through fold and pick up the thread under fabric. Space stitches evenly.

Tack: To secure in place with a couple of handstitches.

Topstitch: A stitch sewn on the Right side of a project.

Tracing wheel: A tool with a handle and a wheel for tracing designs with carbon paper. These can be smooth or serrated.

Walking foot: Used to sew hard-to-feed fabrics, such as fur, and slippery fabrics, such as satin. Check your manual to see if your machine has this foot.

Webbing: Often used for belts (think '70s rainbows), this "strap" trim comes in a variety of widths and colors.

Wrong: The side of the fabric that you don't want shown in the finished project.

Zigzag stitch: It looks as it sounds, like a zigzag. See your machine stitch guide for an example. Smaller widths of a zigzag stitch make a satin stitch, useful for appliqué.

Zipper foot: *See* Cording foot.

Fabric Credits

Where You Sleep:

Reversible Duvet Cover, page 24
Joel Dewberry "Manzanita" in
    Sky Damask

Rainy Day Curtain, page 28
Anna Griffin, Maime (umbrella top)
Betsey Johnson Polka Dots in Teal

Monogram Sham, page 36
Kokka Fabrics, "Ladybugs"

Hangover-Helper Eyeshade, page 42
Amy Butler Nigella in Starflower Tiles
    Spinach
Amy Butler Nigella in Ritzy Stripe Sky

Privacy Pocket Pillow, page 46
Joel Dewberry "Manzanita" in
    Sky Damask

Where You Dress:

Hanging Closet-Organizer, page 56
Amy Butler Pink Coriander

Cosmetics Carryall, page 64
Erin Michael "Loft 1800" for Moda Fabrics

Where You Study:

Tufted Seat Cushion, page 74
Anna Maria, "Chocolate Lollipop" for
    Freespirit Fabrics

Desktop Catchall, page 80
Alexander Henry Fabrics, "Viceroy"

Messenger Book Bag, page 84
Alexander Henry Fabrics, "Grove"

Magritte Pencil Pouch, page 88
Jackie Shapiro "Modern Grace" for
    Windham Fabrics

Where You Hang Out:

Conversation Coasters, page 96
Amy Butler "Lotus" in Tangerine
    Full Moon
Joel Dewberry "Aviary" in Orange Rose
Denyse Schmidt "Katie Jump Rope" in
    Geranium Dots

**Felt Backgammon Board/Checkers
    Board,** page 98
Suzuko Koseki "Suzuko Stripes," for Yuwa

Better Bean Bag, page 100
Jeanne Horton "Worn and Loved c. 1870"
    for Windham Fabrics
Amy Butler "Lotus" in Apricot Wallflower
    for Rowan Fabrics
Suzuko Koseki "Suzuko Stripes" for Yuwa

Amy Butler "Lotus" in Tangerine Full
    Moon
Amy Butler "Lotus" in Yellow Full Moon
    for Rowan Fabrics

Draft Snake, page 104
Alexander Henry Fabrics, "Grove"
Suzuko Koseki "Suzuko Stripes" for Yuwa
Jackie Shapiro "Modern Grace" for Wind
    ham Fabrics

Argyle Fleece Throw, page 106
Hancock Fabrics

Where You Wash:

Laundry Day Backpack, page 110
D's Selection "The Pireued" for Junko
    Matsuda fabrics
Erin Michael "Loft 1800" for Moda Fabrics

Toiletry Tote, page 114
Etsuka Furuya "Leopard" for Echino
    fabrics
LB Krueger "Farmhouse Blues C. 1900"
    for Windham Fabrics
Iron-On Vinyl by Therm O Web

Fuzzy Slippers, page 116
Erin Michael "Loft 1800" for Moda Fabrics

Index